The Polo-Ticks of Life

Arjit Pandey

BlueRose ONE.com
Stories Matter
New Delhi • London

BLUEROSE PUBLISHERS
India | U.K.

BlueRose ONE.com
Stories Matter
New Delhi • London

For permissions requests or inquiries regarding this publication, please contact:

BLUEROSE PUBLISHERS
www.BlueRoseONE.com
info@bluerosepublishers.com
+91 8882 898 898
+4407342408967

ISBN: 978-93-6261-109-3

Cover design: Arjit Pandey & Tahira
Typesetting: Tanya Raj Upadhyay

First Edition: May 2024

TABLE OF CONTENTS

INTRODUCTION:

Have you ever felt confused in your life? Have you ever felt alone? Have you ever experienced total emptiness? Have you ever cried for someone? Have you ever faced depression in your work life or academics? Have you ever felt frustrated with your parents, relatives, or friends?

If yes, then read this book I am sure you will find your answers.

Let's conduct a science experiment called the blind spot experiment.

Here is a dot on the left and a cross on the right. Shut your right eye and look directly at the cross with your left eye. Keep focused on the cross, and the dot will vanish now turn the book back and forth while still holding the focus. You shall see the dot coming and receding.

Then cover your left eye with your hand and focus your right eye on the dot. As you focus on the dot, the cross vanishes.

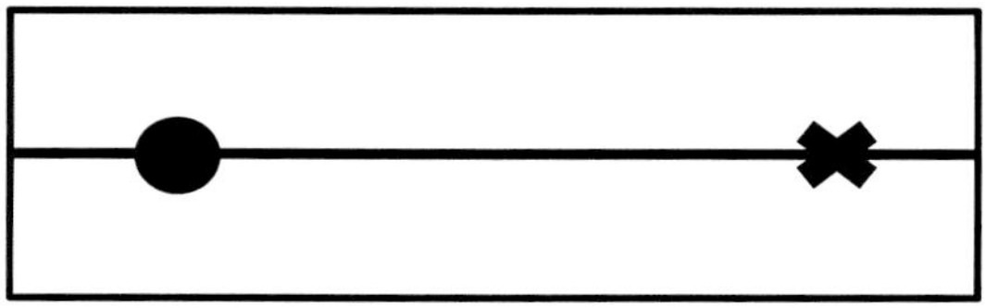

Now, we have drawn a line across the dot and cross. Now, repeat the same experiment and you will find that when the dot or cross disappears, the line drawn does not disappear.

I'm not going into the technical details of this experiment, but the simple logic is that your eye can perceive both positivity (dot) and negativity (cross). If you want to focus on either the dot or the cross, you have to close one eye, either the positive or the negative. That's how you can focus on either the positive side of life or the negative side of life.

However, many people connect the positive side and negative side with a line of equilibrium, and they try to get motivated by seeing that line.

Many times, when someone gets trapped in difficulties, whether it's relationship problems, issues in the office work culture, conflicts with parents, or any other challenge, they often wonder why these troubles are happening to them specifically.

Do you realize that these problems represent negative vibrations? According to Newton's third law, every action has an equal and opposite reaction. Therefore, if you are experiencing these negative vibrations now, it implies that you might have generated negative vibrations earlier, which is why you are facing them today.

You might say, "No, I am very positive, I never do that." But let's recall: Have you ever trolled someone over social media, or found amusement in someone else's trolling or bad jokes? Have you ever engaged in gossip about your friends or teachers? Have you ever made negative remarks about food while dining at a restaurant? Have you criticized movies or anyone in your life?

There lived a girl who shared her room with another girl. Whenever she talked to someone, she revealed all the information about her roommate—what her roommate did that day, what she had worn, what shades of lipstick she used, and how she did her makeup. She complained every day that her room was always noisy owing to her roommate's phone calls with her boyfriend, whom she would always refer to as Pullu.

Today, her roommate's boyfriend had brought her a makeup kit, which made her roommate completely stunned because she couldn't imagine ever receiving such a gift in her life.

Later that day, her roommate left to watch a movie with her boyfriend and came back at 3 am.

Despite telling her mom that she was going to study, her roommate was going to meet her boyfriend.

She was also envious, wondering why she did not have a boyfriend with whom she could go out and also receive gifts.

Her roommate broke up with her boyfriend, and she was crying

She was generating the bad vibes by calling her roommate a jerk, and as a result, she pulled similar situations into her life. She soon found a boy approaching her, and they became boyfriend and girlfriend. After a while, she realized she had manifested such situations through the criticism of her roommate.

She was creating negative vibrations by criticizing her roommate, and later she experienced the same, as stated in Newton's third law.

Negative things provide a sense of temporary relief, which is often what we seek in life. Happiness is our ultimate goal, and we always look for easier paths to achieve it. While negative things may be detrimental in the long run, they offer momentary happiness, and we often overlook their negative impact. On the other hand, positive actions seem appealing but are challenging to incorporate into our daily lives. For instance, when you come across a positive quote that motivates you to enact positive change, you may attempt to integrate it into your routine to become a better person. However, sustaining this positivity proves difficult over time. Many of us give up because it requires perseverance, and results aren't immediately evident. Although positive actions yield positive results, patience is key. If you're patient and willing to endure the challenges associated with positivity, nothing can hinder your progress.

The human brain exhibits a natural inclination to amplify negative experiences or interactions over positive ones, a phenomenon known as negativity bias, leading individuals to fixate on a single negative event amidst a plethora of positive occurrences.

Negative emotions typically prompt deeper contemplation and more thorough processing than positive ones. It's common for us to possess a richer vocabulary to articulate negative thoughts compared to positive ones. Consequently, negative emotions, memories, feedback, and impressions carry greater weight and impact on our cognition.

Don't succumb to fleeting happiness by engaging in trolling, gossiping, discussing others' relationships, or criticizing your manager or boss. I understand it's challenging, but trust me, once you break free from these traps, you'll discover lasting happiness and peace.

Stop gossiping and criticizing

When I started working as a political consultant, I tried to understand how common people think. I visited many houses in villages, I talked to them, I understood their thought process, and I was witnessed to their innocence. Surprisingly, I found that people easily accept negative vibrations. Understanding this psychology, marketers, and consultants change the entire game of marketing.

I remember how the opposition party won the election by using negative marketing against a well-known political leader. Through negative marketing, they portrayed the well-known political leader as lacking knowledge of politics and being unable to handle any situation. As a result, people began to question his competence as a political leader. These negative campaigns were run repeatedly, leading people to perceive the well-known political leader as incompetent.

Many leaders spread negative content through social media and verbal communication because they know that people enjoy such content and would spread it further. This thought process played a significant role in marketing.

But people don't always grasp the concept of resonance, which beautifully explains that if A and B are two different bodies with the same frequency, when A generates vibrations, whether positive or negative, B will start generating the same vibrations as A. That's how vibrations attract each other.

Suppose A, B, C, ..., Z are people who enjoy negative content, meaning they have the same frequency. If A thinks that his luck isn't working, there's sadness in his life, and he feels alone, then A's vibration will begin to impact B, C, ..., Z, and they will start thinking similarly.

If you enjoy gossiping about your friends, participating in office gossip, deriving pleasure from others' unhappiness, trolling others, or sharing negative posts on social media or WhatsApp, then you are also attracting negative vibrations into your life.

There was a girl who excelled in her studies and topped her board exams. When she achieved this, the media visited her house to interview her, and the interview was shared on social media. However, instead of appreciating her accomplishments, people started trolling her for her facial hair.

During the interview, she expressed, "If I had scored a few marks lower, I might not have become famous. Maybe that would have been better. I'm not too bothered by the situation because I've faced this for a long time. People find it strange to see girls with facial hair because they're not accustomed to it. However, I'm okay with how God has made me. For those who see a difference, it doesn't matter. Even Chanakya was trolled, and he didn't care. Similarly, I won't let it affect me and will focus on my studies."

Her mother also shared her feelings during the interview, saying, "It hurt to see my daughter being trolled on social media. Many people said hurtful things about her. I advised my daughter not to let it affect her.

Before diving into this book, clear your mind of all negative thoughts. Begin to cultivate a positive mindset and express gratitude towards your parents, family, siblings, teachers, relatives, the universe, and God. Doing so will yield positive results.

Stop Attracting Negative Vibrations

I do believe that what we imagine can become real if our thoughts are clear and focused. Most of my days passed in contemplation under the patronizing gaze of Allahabad University's grand buildings. I would often find myself tracing my fingertips along the contours of stone structures, daydreaming within the hallowed halls of academia. There, standing among the student population in the vibrant tapestry of academia, I dreamt of a future where I would drink thirstily from the wellspring of knowledge and life experiences that lay ahead of me, waiting to be tasted.

With each ensuing visit to the university, my mind would translate into the future: I was once again a student, in lively debate, and engrossed in the intellectual pursuits that would define the very essence of Allahabad University. Such a dream inspired me on further steps in life, and the realization that the future was laid out before me filled me with inspiration and purpose. And then, after what seemed like the guiding light of the clarity of my imagination and conviction in my heart, I was admitted to Allahabad University, and it was a conviction that with the strength of will and a definite course in one's life, dreams could indeed become realities.

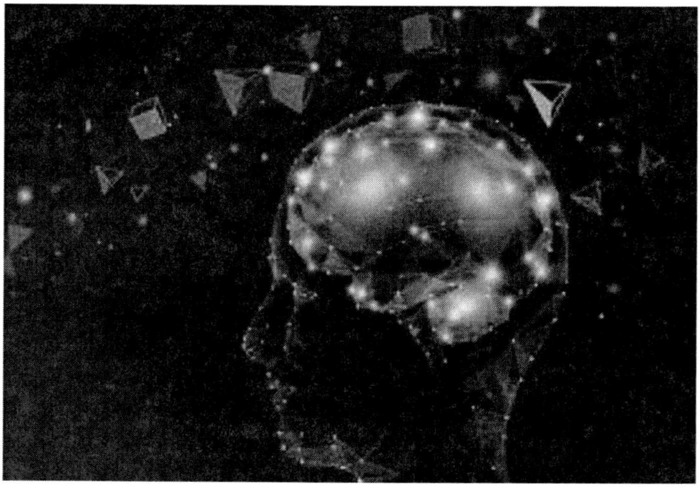

Engage in imagination. Spend your time envisioning positive scenarios. Though it may be challenging at first, strive to focus on positive imaginings.

In retrospect, my journey from envisioning myself as a student at Allahabad University to actually stepping on its campus turned out to be a poignant reminder of that deep connection between imagination and achievement. It strongly reinforced my belief in the inherent potency of visualization and affirmed that with a resolute mind and unwavering faith, the possibilities that lie within the realm of our imagination are boundless.

With the shift from Allahabad University to the prestigious institution of IIT Delhi came a new chapter in my journey, the power of imagination had shaped it. I could not help but often get pulled into that aura of excellence and innovation that pervaded the atmosphere while visiting the IIT Delhi campus. I used to close my eyes in such moments and get captured within the palpable energy of the institution as if I felt what it would feel like to be within such an institution of repute.

At every visit, my aspirations grew stronger, fueled by the vivid imagery of success and achievement conjured in my mind. It was almost like I could taste the happiness that would come with the beginning of a new academic journey—surrounded by brilliant minds, and thrown into the culture of intellectual curiosity. And then, apparently guided by the unrelenting clarity of my vision, my dreams turned into reality, and I found myself welcomed into the folds of IIT Delhi as a student.

Acknowledge the power of imagination.

The realization of this dream became an emotional reminder of how close imagination and manifestation were. It affirmed my belief in the power of visualization and ensured me that if that determination was accentuated with a steady focus, nothing was beyond attainment—not even the highest of my goals. Moving ahead with new beginnings to my academic life, I carried with me the lessons from the experiences and was so grateful to have had the opportunity to turn my dreams into achievements.

Imagination Manifestation

> Imagination is akin to planting a seed: envisioning yourself gaining admission to a prestigious institute. Manifestation, then, is the fruition of that seed—embracing the reality of your admission and aligning your actions accordingly, resulting in feelings of joy and fulfillment.

After finishing my studies at IIT, I stood at the crossroads of life wondering where to go and what to do for the rest of my life. As a design and development engineer, I had started at the beginning of my career, but soon I realized that I couldn't find the passion and fulfillment I was expecting from the profession. The vast emptiness and the burning desire to pursue my vocation or my calling in life put me at the edge.

In this vein, I was left with the college complexities of self-discovery and personal fulfillment, searching for my passion and purpose. It appeared, quite ironically, to be an elusive journey meted with uncertainty and self-doubt. My best efforts, though, in sorting out some clarity and direction, resulted in a maze of conflicting feelings and societal expectations, not knowing which turn to turn or which path to follow.

Amidst all this existential crisis, I was not alone; my contemporaries too were lost, desperately trying to chart out their destinies amidst the screaming din of societal norms and personal aspirations. Each of us embarked on a pilgrimage in search of the many threads of our innermost desires and ambitions.

Though challenges and uncertain situations loomed ahead, I found clarity and purpose through the light. With a resilient spirit and an indomitable heart, I embarked on a journey of self-exploration, having an inner conviction that my paths would be illuminated by the light that would guide me through to fulfillment and meaning waiting for me on this journey. Though the road ahead would have many twists and turns, I set out on this journey with unshakable hope and optimism that every step taken brought me closer to the realization of my true calling and destiny.

So, I began my businesses, and unfortunately, they did not yield the expected outcomes. Then, I stepped into the world of startups, where I gained a lot of experience and learned a lot about how things work. I later moved into the role of a political consultant, and this was the pinnacle of my career. However, even at the peak of my career, I remained unsatisfied and miserable in that particular environment. I decided to take the bold step and walk away from the cushion of my well-paying job and embark on this journey of writing and documenting everything. I wanted to document how I overcame difficulties and triumph when I needed it the most, and possibly inspire others through my journey. The default uncertainties and foreseeable pitfalls did not deter me from taking that step because I was very confident in myself, my talents, and this truly allowed me to walk out of the familiar into the pursuit of my passions.

A lot of us are looking for the true meaning of our lives. Sometimes, we have everything, but we just feel incomplete. We cannot feel it on our skin, but we know it, and because of this, we are sad too.

Many questions arise in our mind like:

Who am I?

Why am I here?

What is the purpose of my life?

No other creature on earth has this ability.

These answers are difficult to discover for sure, but I'll give you a hint;

We are an eternal Soul only temporarily within a human body to experience karmic reflections while learning how to not create them. We are also here to discover our oneness with all of creation by learning to value life in all its forms as much as we do our own.

Concept of Soul and Body:

Great Scientist Albert Einstein explained the relationship between energy and Mass. Energy mass equivalence is a concept in physics that says energy and mass are related and can be converted into each other. It's famously represented by Einstein's equation, E=mc^2, where E stands for energy, m stands for mass, and c is the speed of light. This equation means that even a small amount of mass can contain a huge amount of energy, and vice versa. So, it tells us that mass and energy are interchangeable and that they're essentially two sides of the same coin.

Our System is also made up of Soul and Body, soul is energy and body is mass.

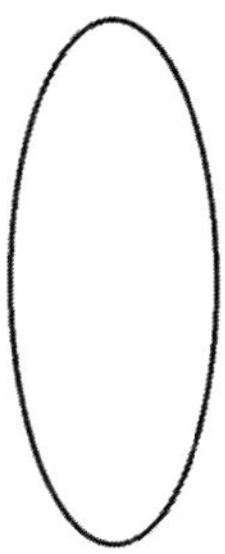

Soul

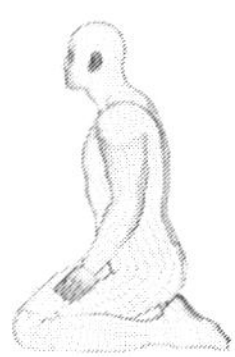

Body

Soul= Energy

Body= Mass

Human System== Soul+Body

Body is made up of five elements-

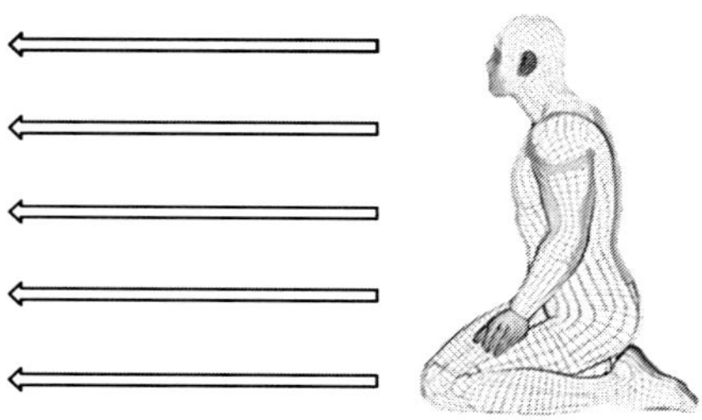

Earth (Solid)

Water (Liquid)

Fire (Plasma)

Space (Ether)

Air (Gas)

The five elements of the human body each symbolize a different aspect of life and health, much like the various states of matter in science.

1. Earth(solid state) : This symbolizes strength, stability, and physical body structure. It is associated with bones, muscles, and tissues.
2. Water(liquid state) : It symbolizes fluidity, flexibility, and emotional balance. It governs bodily fluids such as blood, saliva, and lymph.

3. Fire(plasma state) : This symbolizes change, energy, and metabolism. It governs digestion, body heat, and energy use.
4. Space(ether) : It symbolizes expansion, connection, and the space in the body. It includes subtle energy pathways such as nadis.
5. Air(gas state): : It relates to motion, communication, and vitality. It is the ultimate director of breathing, circulation, and the nervous system.

In the Bhagavad Gita, it is stated that the Atma (Soul) is never made nor destroyed; it just changes its body. Curiously, modern scientists have also explained it in a similar manner.

Scientists proposed the law of conservation of energy. The law states that energy cannot be created or destroyed; instead, it changes its form.

Soul is made up of energies and vibrations-

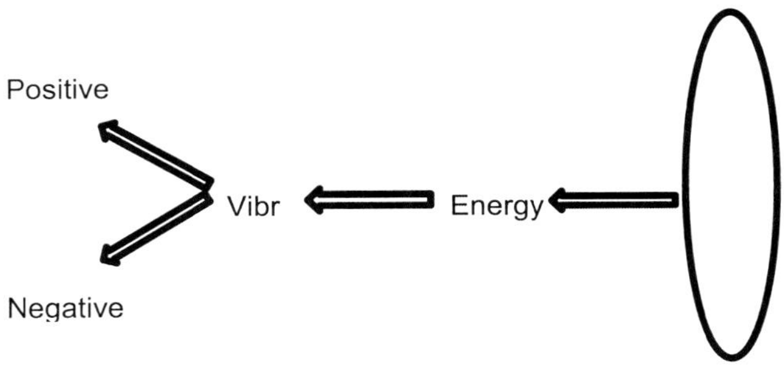

Soul

Our body consists of five elements, and when you are hurt or get injured, your nerves send messages to your brain, letting it know that something's wrong, making you feel pain. To stop the pain, you might take medicine or have surgery.

BUT

When you surround yourself with negative vibrations, you can get depressed, and sometimes, people may even resort to suicide if they cannot cope with these negative feelings. Negative vibrations are directly linked to the soul, and you cannot manage negative vibrations unless you learn the correct way to handle it. The following chapters are going to explore the explanation of how to handle negative vibrations.

Summary:

- Human System is made up of Soul and Body
- The body is made up of five elements
- Soul is made up of Energy and Vibrations
- Acknowledge the power of imagination.
- Use your imagination to think about good things happening. It might be hard at first, but try to focus on positive thoughts.

CHAPTER -1

THE MASTERMIND

In thermodynamics, the second law provides a comprehensive explanation of the functioning of heat engines and elucidates the fundamental concepts of heat sources and sinks.

The source can be likened to the mastermind, represented by a divine entity like God, which provides energies essential for our existence, growth, and sustenance. Conversely, the sink embodies our soul, acting as the receptor and absorber of these energies, guiding and influencing our journey. Meanwhile, the engine symbolizes our physical body, serving as the vessel through which these energies manifest and interact with the world around us.

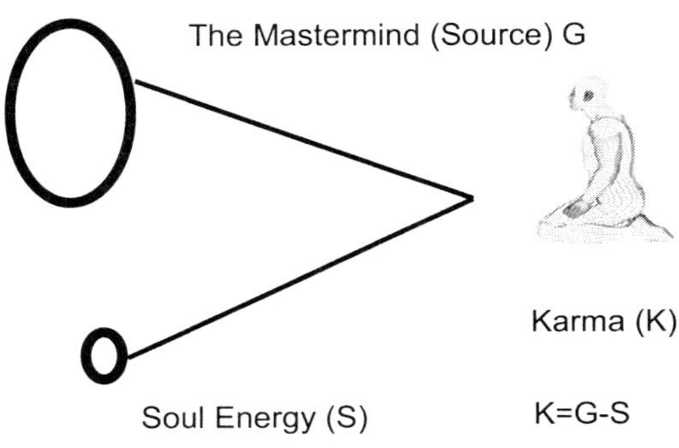

The Mastermind, symbolized by God, grants a fraction of His energy to our physical bodies, and it is through the actions and activities of our body that our karma is determined. Our karma, in essence, reflects the utilization of our soul's energy—whether we choose to harbor positive or negative thoughts and intentions towards others.

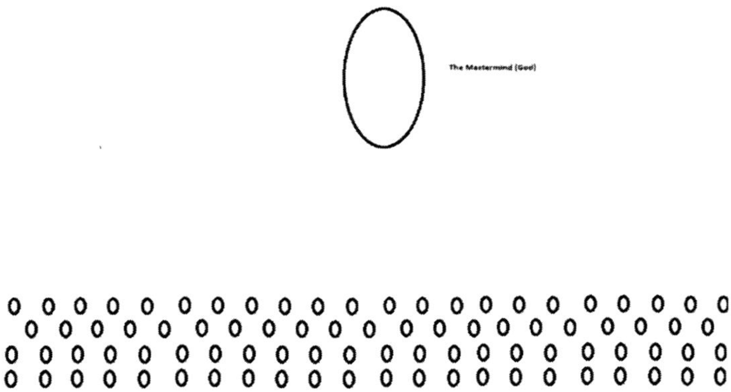

Accept the existence of GOD

Life is a big game board, and every step we take and every decision we make brings a story that unfolds. In this complicated plot, we have to cross experiences on the journey of life—in moments of elation and sorrow, of success and failure. But we are never devoid of God's help. The divine hand of God is by our side, patting our hearts in moments of heartbreak and sharing in our jubilee in moments of victory. He gives purpose and meaning to every moment, showing us which way to turn as the light of God's wisdom guides us toward enlightenment and fulfillment. So, in the traversing of the labyrinth of life, we find reassurance that the light of God's guidance is always by our side, leading us toward enlightenment and fullness.

These are moments of shining happiness that are always there in life, tapping the experiences and feelings of a person. In the grand weaving of life, where thousands of threads interweave, we often move through moments of extreme happiness with such ease, lighting up our pathway and filling our hearts with joy and contentment to such a level that they redefine it. These beacons of light guide us through the labyrinth of existence and provide solace and inspiration in the midst of so many challenges and uncertainties that we must endure.

Yet in all these glorious experiences, sometimes it feels like there is an unexpected shadow of sadness that comes down upon us, shrouding our spirits in darkness and driving us deep into the unfathomable mysteries of human existence. It is during these times of sorrow that, although unwelcome, act as poignant reminders that life is by its nature unpredictable and that we always remain in the face of impermanence and change.

We find ourselves face to face with life's duality in moments of joy and pain, all interlaced in the mosaic of experiences that make up our journey in this world. It is in this complex ballet of emotions where we find the deepest level of the human experience as we navigate highs and lows with resilience, grace, and unwavering determination.

Thus, as we weave our way through the tapestry of life, let us open our hearts to every moment with a firm spirit, knowing that it is in the contrast of joy and sorrow that we find meaning, purpose, and thus, true humanity.

When the burden of desolation weighs heavily on our hearts, when despair threatens to break us, we turn to the reassuring presence of God, finding comfort and refuge in His arms. When our spirits are wrapped up in the thick blanket of sorrow, it is often an unexpected glimmer of hope that rises from the ashes, like a gentle breeze in the storm, which, though warming and comforting, frees us from the oppressive burden of sorrow and leads us along a path lightened by the promise of better days to come. With every ray of hope, unexpected as it may be, the human spirit shows its resilience and its boundless capacity for grace and redemption, comforting and strengthening us in this intricate dance of life. Basking in the light of this newfound hope, we are reminded that within each of us is a wellspring of strength and grace that we can draw upon as we navigate the intricacies of our life's journey.

You cannot win with the mastermind.

Does God Exist?

A spiritual writer had shared his story of how he became a spiritual writer. He had two near-death experiences in his life, brought on by a serious medical issue that cut off his breathing tube. He thought that he was unconscious for less than ten seconds each time. His wife witnessed each event and shook him back to consciousness. The experiences were initiated by coughing fits that he had that cut off his air supply.

While he was unconscious he was very clearly out of his body, and he saw the long tunnel with a bright light at the end. At the end of the tunnel, he saw hundreds of smiling people in the vividly bright white and gold surroundings, beckoning him to cross over to the "other side". He did not recognize any of the people, but He was floating through the tunnel towards them. Then He heard his wife calling his name, and he turned around and went back to her.

He was convinced that for both of these near-death experiences, it was his soul personality that was traveling along the tunnels. If he had not been summoned back to his body, he was sure that he would have proceeded along to that blissful-looking state of death.

It takes less than ten seconds for him to be dead for his soul personality to leave his body. By that he means that in well under a minute he would have made the transition to continue life on the spiritual plane, on the "other side".

He was very thankful to his wife, for rescuing him, and to his family and friends who supported him through prayer.

Now he is a 70-year-old man who researches and writes on spiritual matters. So he is grateful to have had these experiences.

In this realm of human inquiry and understanding, a striking paradox emerges when discussing the idea of the divine. Many, who have delved into the deepest theological debates and philosophical reflections, often ask a core question: if there is a divine being, then why is He invisible and not seen by our senses? This skepticism, stemming from the principles of empiricism and rational inquiry, is perhaps most typical of those who have been plunged into the depths of knowledge and understanding.

Indeed, it is perfectly understandable why people, especially those trained and ensconced in scientific pursuits, tend to pay immense value to tangible evidence and empirical observation. In a world that is driven by cause and effect, where concepts are tested against experiment and proven through observable results, the idea of embracing something as profound as the belief in the existence of God based on faith alone is a tough sell.

Yet, amidst this skepticism, it is interesting to point out a significant irony within human cognition: while many doubt the idea of a divine being because it cannot be directly seen, they freely acknowledge and accept scientific theories, that posit the existence of even more abstract and hidden entities. Take, for instance, the case of fundamental particles like electrons, protons, and neutrons—the very building blocks of matter, in modern physics. These particles lie outside the realm of direct human perception, but they play a crucial role in our comprehension of the universe. Although these same particles are accepted and embraced because they are entities inferred through complex theoretical structures and validated through indirect observation and experimental evidence.

It essentially creates a beautiful contrast between belief systems: the disbelief in the existence of God, since there appears to be no observable evidence for him, versus the acceptability of scientific theories whose source was on things that weren't directly observable by the human eye. That is the essence of this dichotomy, wherein it identifies the complexity associated with faith and reason and the complexities that come with each.

Therefore, although, understandably, humans might doubt the existence of a god as they follow an empirical norm, so should the openness to the limitations of human perception and the mysteries that lie beyond the boundaries of what science is allowed to research. In that sense, it makes us a richer perception of existence as we embrace the empirical and the ineffable, the concrete and the transcendent, in our search for meaning and understanding in the universe.

Let's use an example:

Case-1 knocking over a table with your fingers and hearing the sound through your ears without putting your head into the table. And

Case-2 knocking over a table with your fingers and listening to the sound while putting your ear directly on the table.

In both cases, you'll notice that you perceive two distinct types of sound, despite applying the same force with your fingers. Why does this occur?

The difference lies in the connection between your vibration and the vibration of the table. When you knock on the table, your fingers transmit vibrations to the table's surface. As a result, when you hear the sound while putting your ear on the table, you're not only perceiving the sound waves but also feeling the vibrations that have been transferred to the table.

You connect your vibration with the table's vibration when you feel the vibration generated by your finger while knocking. Similarly, to perceive the existence of God, you must connect your vibration with God's vibration. This connection allows you to sense the presence of God.

How do you match your vibration with the Mastermind (God)?

God is the source of energy, or one might say He is the supreme soul. To connect with God, you must align yourself with your own energy.

The human structure comprises both body and soul, representing matter and energy, respectively. As God is the ultimate source of energy, aligning with His vibration entails activating your soul energy to resonate in harmony with God.

To activate your soul energy, begin by sitting and concentrating your mind on a specific point, envisioning it as the source of energy. Initially, focus on this point with your eyes open, then gradually close your eyes and continue to concentrate. As you immerse yourself in this practice, aim to align your vibration with that of God. Engage in a dialogue with Him, communicating your thoughts and intentions. Over time, you will begin to sense a profound energy emanating from within, and you may find that your problems start to resolve themselves.

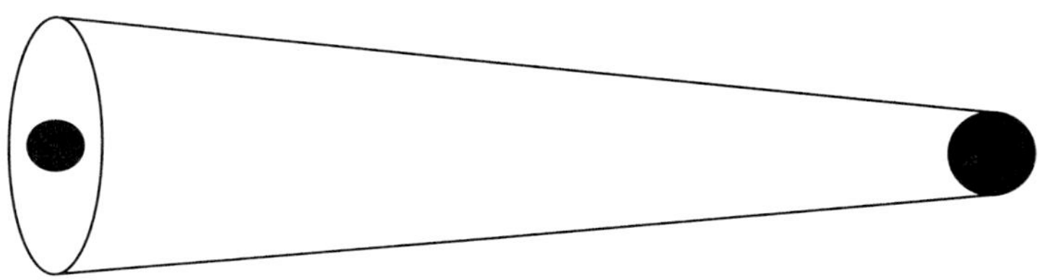

The Art of Matching Vibration-

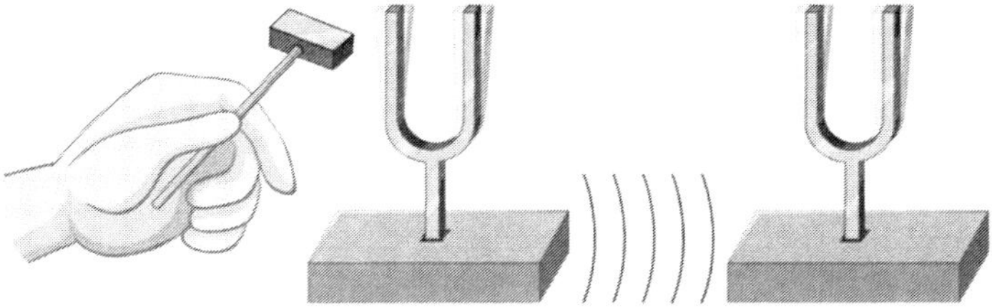

When we observe two tuning forks sharing identical frequencies, an intriguing phenomenon unfolds: upon striking the first tuning fork, the second one spontaneously initiates vibrations, despite the absence of any direct physical interaction. This fascinating occurrence serves as a poignant illustration of how vibrations can harmonize and synchronize seamlessly when they resonate at precisely the same frequency, offering a profound insight into the interconnected nature of vibrational energy.

> Make your frequency align with God's through meditation; in doing so, you'll synchronize your positive vibrations with others.

But to really know how to align vibrations, one has to plunge into the deep understanding of how both positive and negative vibrations intricately shape our environment that surrounds us. It becomes apparent in this study that the energies we emit and absorb play a vital role in shaping what comes as our experiences and outcomes. Whereas positive vibrations radiate harmony, abundance, and growth, negative vibrations breed discord, limitation, and stagnation. Thus, it is vital to see the profound impact of negative vibrations and the critical importance of creating distance from their detrimental influence within the framework of getting ahead in life.

Here, we are talking about situations that could possibly arise in any household.

Case-1

Son: Dad, I wish to become a photographer.

Dad: Photography? But we've spent so much on your education to ensure your success in life.

Son: I know, Dad, but photography brings me so much joy and accomplishment.

Dad: No, just complete your engineering and get a job. After that, you can do anything you want.

Case-2

Parent: Why aren't you getting married?

He/She: I want to focus on my dreams.

Parent: What will society say? We can afford to arrange your marriage.

He/She: Please give me some time.

Parent: No, we've decided to arrange your marriage this December. We are already looking for a bride/groom for you.

The occurrence of 5-6 suicides within our college community due to my tenure in IIT greatly disturbed me. I was confronted with deep questions of what might have ensued in the minds of those individuals who were clearly well-educated and enrolled in one of the most prestigious institutions, to resort to such extreme measures.

These individuals could not.

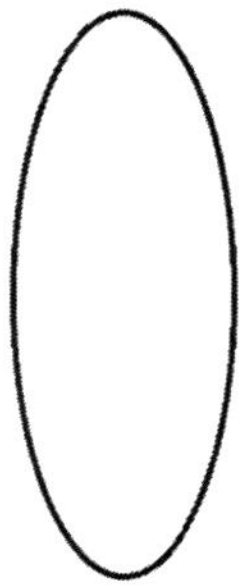

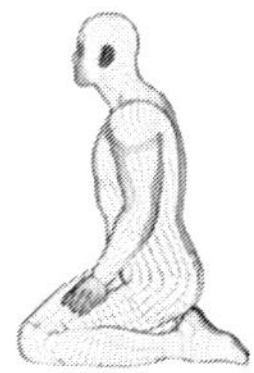

Soul Body

The body can hurt, feel stressed, and be anxious, but the soul, being energy, acts as a source of healing to overcome challenges.

To subside the negative vibrations, there is a need to positively create everything that happens in life. It really strengthens the relationship with your children because, in a warm, nurturing atmosphere, the love makes the family feel close and beautiful. The same goes for students who hold a positive stance towards exams and career prospects, having an increased amount of motivation to get into learning and growth. As a job seeker or a corporate employee, positive thoughts about career prospects and colleagues create a supportive and harmonious work environment, subsequently increasing productivity and giving a satisfactory life. Consciously merging personal vibration with positivity and hope invites possibilities and a wholesome life journey.

By creating a positive environment around you, you merge your vibration with positivity.

This way, you attract positive results and experiences into your life.

To merge the vibration with positivity and God

1. **Sit in a meditation position.**
2. **Close your eyes**
3. **Inhale and imagine that you are drawing positivity into your body.**
4. **Exhale and imagine that you are releasing negativity.**
5. **Do not think negatively about any individual.**
6. **Talk to God.**

Remember, the art of matching vibrations only works if you do not think negatively about any individual or anything.

Summary-

- The Mastermind, whom you can call God, is the supreme power and source of energy.
- When you feel low, align your vibration with Him, talk to Him, and ask Him to increase your energy level.
- You can achieve everything if you understand the art of matching vibrations with others.
- The art of matching vibrations only works if you don't think negatively about any person or anything.

CHAPTER-2

CONFUSION

Look at these pictures. While they remain stable in reality, they appear to be moving to you. Additionally, upon closer inspection, you will notice that the colorful images seem to move faster than the black and white ones.

Picture-1 Images designed by Freepik

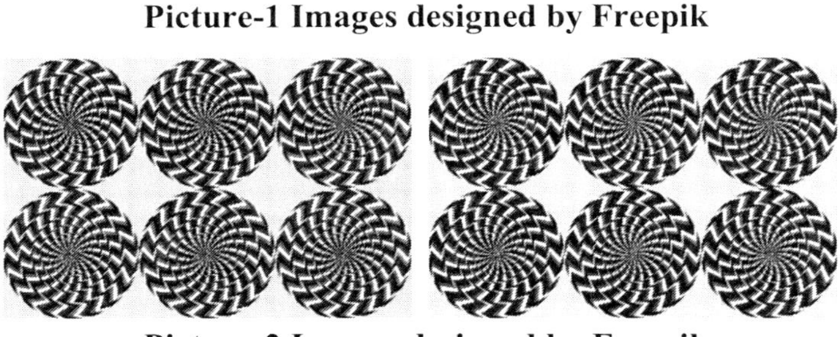

Picture-2 Images designed by Freepik

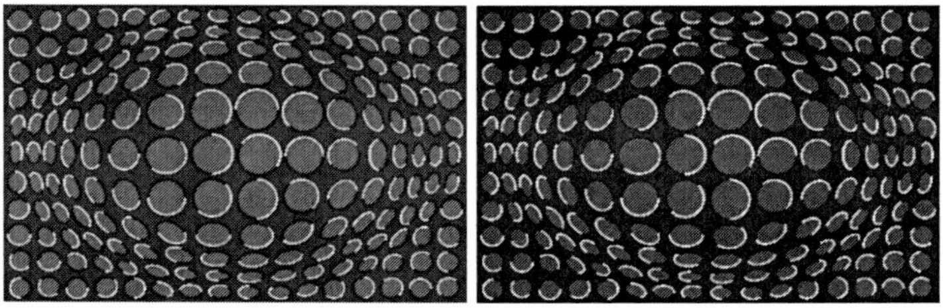

Picture-3 Images designed by Freepik

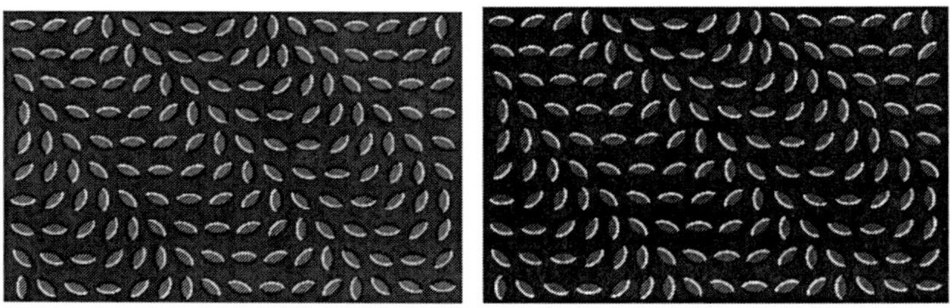

Picture-4 Images designed by Freepik

You are experiencing the motion because there exists a coordination failure between the eye and brain, and this leads to confusion. The information reported by the eye contradicts information by the brain. This is just one example of the fact that what we see may not always be an accurate representation of reality.

Yes, I am confused. The confusion has struck me many times throughout my life and it did call for deep reflection. I am sure you too have at some point in time experienced moments of confusion. We must, when confusion ensues, confront it head-on and accept it. We should not pretend to be tough by hiding our vulnerability behind fake forms of strength. We must accept our confusion as a normal part of being human. Only then can we set on a road of exploration and development.

Do you believe that Thomas Alva Edison went through more than one thousand failures before eventually inventing the electric bulb? In fact, I believe that Edison went through countless cases of confusion and failure before finally coming up with a working design for the electric bulb.

As a child, I thought I would become an engineer because of my family members who became engineers. But by growing older, my ambitions changed, and I was developing great desires to become a scientist. After some time, my thoughts turned in another direction and, at present, I do not know what I am going to be. I am not the only one going through such a phase of life; as you read this, you are also experiencing the same doubts about one's future, about the path to success, happiness, and finding the right roadmap to fulfillment.

Which One to Choose:

So, you get confused if there are too many options:

My friend went to find a suitable groom for her marriage pretty often and usually, she came to ask my advice and share her experiences with me. But after every meeting with a prospective groom, she got more puzzled and confused with her decision.

She: "Why did he give me chocolate?"

Me: "Maybe it is his way of greeting."

She: "No, I think he is an experienced girl-finder, so he knows exactly how to please the girl."

Rejected

She: "Why did he call me at midnight?"

Me: "Maybe he was busy with his work."

She: "No, I think he is an experienced girl-talker, so he has a habit of talking to girls at midnight."

Rejected

She: "I first met a guy for my marriage, he gave me a chocolate, but this one didn't give me anything."

Me: "Maybe it is his way of greeting."

She: "No, I think he is a rude guy by nature."

Rejected

Since she has many options, every time she meets a guy, she gets confused. But the decision of marrying someone is a tough decision and also an informative decision. You have to read a person's character, and take time to understand them. If you have clarity about your expectations from your future husband or wife, you won't get confused. But if you do not have clarity about your expectations about your future husband or wife, you will get confused every time.

Every time I order food using one of the food delivery apps, I become so confused. Hunger pangs bombard me, and I desperately feel the need to stuff my belly. The huge choice about what to fill my stomach overwhelms me into a state of confusion that makes me a bit crazy about not knowing what would be best to fill my hunger and nourish myself.

When presented with too many options, one often feels paralyzed and confused and makes poor decisions. It happens not only in ordering food via delivery app but also in many other parts of life where multiple options are presented for consideration and evaluation.

Whenever you feel paralyzed, the key to solving whatever it is that's troubling you is taking a step back and looking at the situation objectively. You need to pinpoint the cause of your confusion and define your goals and priorities. You need all the information that pertains to the situation, and you need to weigh the consequences of each of your options. You can consult with trusted friends or family or call mentors for their opinion.

Whenever you feel confused about what to order, you're just wasting time by scrolling. Ask a friend, call your parents, and ask them what's for dinner to order that meal.

Whenever it pertains to food, your tastes align with you and your family or friend's vibration, so you have no problem asking a friend or family member to guide or suggest options. But ultimately, the decision is yours, so the choice is yours.

But what if you're feeling confused in a difficult situation and not getting support from a family or friend?

Then what will you do?

Connect with the mastermind, talk to Him, let your problems out, and ask for help.

Trust me, you'll get whatever it is you need.

"Life is replete with variations, and the way you perceive life greatly hinges on your level of maturity. "Maturity comes with age."

Oh, sorry, I might be wrong; there are many people who display maturity early in life.

There was a 13-year-old boy who had been living with his father; unfortunately, his mother did not share his home. His mother appeared to be an ambitious girl, or maybe she just gave an appearance of ambition.

When I asked him he talked about the quantum world, he liked old songs and he liked to discuss life issues. I was really surprised how a 13-year-old boy can think like this. When I was talking to him, he had raised topics such as the quantum world, while also liking old songs and discussing life issues. I was really surprised at how a 13-year-old boy can sound so mature.

He grew up too early because his mom did not give him love. Due to the absence of love and affection, his mind started functioning differently and created a vacuum. To fill that vacuum, he had started thinking like an adult man.

Think about your feeling of vacuity; when you are all alone, you are likely to think like a philosopher.

Now, the story starts with a man who battled his inner vacuity and sought love to fill the spaces inside. But he was cheated upon, heartbroken, and there he was once again—alone. Despite all the pain of his past, he had the courage to seek love once again, only to be cheated once again.

My father once asked me, "What do you want to become in your life?"

Caught in the act, and without any clear idea in my mind, I hastily said that I wanted to become an engineer to avoid any argument.

But deep down, I did not know the path of my life, and I did not know what I actually wanted.

The journey of my life started with confusion. As I got the notion to start going to school, I always found myself wondering about the need for it.

Questions arose in my mind: Why do we go to school?

Why do we obey laws and customs?

In the Mahabharata, during the war, Arjuna was confused on the battlefield, amidst the cacophony of war, Arjuna, the valiant warrior and central character, was faced with a severe inner dilemma.

He was torn between whether to fight or not. Seeing his own kin and beloved masters ranged against him, Arjuna was perplexed by the moral quandary of having to fight those whom he considered dear and worthy of respect.

So he sought advice from Krishna who guided him and gave him clarity and solved all his confusion over life, war and karma.

Whenever you feel confused you need a mentor who can guide you to get clarity. But to find a good mentor is very tough. So make God your mentor, try to match your vibration with God and pray to him to mentor you.

Summary:

- Confusion is part of everyone's life; just accept when you're confused.
- If you are confused, you can seek guidance from your family or friends.

- But if you're confused during a tough situation and not receiving support from family or friends, connect with the Mastermind (GOD), talk to Him, share your problems, and ask for help. Trust me, you'll get what you need.

CHAPTER - 3

CONFIDENCE

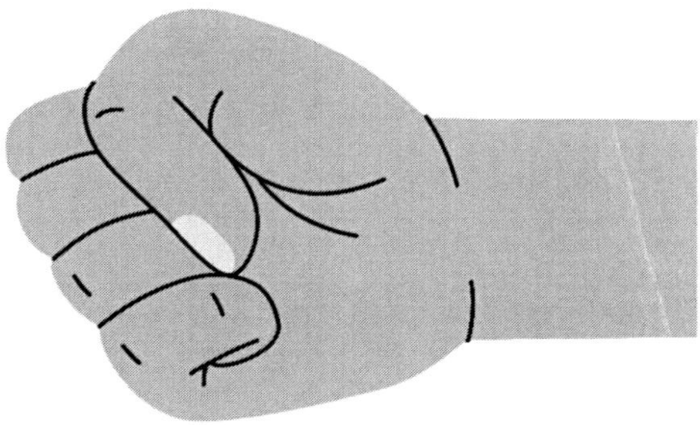

Many encourage one to gain confidence, but the question comes up: how to do it? Your imagination can help establish confidence within you but always remember to include God with it. Seek God's help to increase your confidence

Starting up to confidence, start by praying for strength and guidance. As you go along in your journey, do not think of the negative self-talk but of positive affirmations. Question any irrational beliefs that might tie you up and replace them with your inner strength and ability. Treat yourself with kindness and kindness, especially when you fail or stumble because there is an imperfection in humans that, in fact, is useful for learning and growing. Dream of yourself as having accomplished things, and let this picture be upheld with positive affirmations. Besides all your efforts, appeal to God to give you the confidence you want and to help you overcome any uncertainty or insecurity that may find their way in your life. Believe in the work of God that is unfolding for you and trust that He is beside you in every step you take.

Allow your worries and anxieties to be taken care of by God, knowing that He is beside you with every stride.

Include in your faith affirmations such as "I am confident in God's plan for me" or "With God's help, I can face every hardship" for confidence. Also, cultivate a grateful attitude for God for the thousands of blessings and opportunities He gives you. If you are concentrating on your blessings and strengths, you can develop a sense of confidence that is also grounded in your faith and gratitude and will help you approach life's challenges courageously and with strength of resilience.

When I came to IIT during my college days, this was my first examination experience. A surprise quiz took me through a state in which I was taken aback. The result was shocking; I got only zero out of 10 points. However, I had faith in myself; I did not let this failure mess with my confidence levels. Instead, it turned into a mission to regain my confidence level and reinforce it.

To regain my confidence level, I dove deeper into believing in myself. I, therefore, turned to prayer, seeking comfort and guidance from a higher power, finding solace in the assurance of divine support. At the same time, I realized the urgent need for discipline in my daily habits. I then resolved that success comes through discipline in routine activities. This led me to initiate a transformative shift by visiting the library regularly; for me, the library is a sanctuary of knowledge and opportunity.

Within the calm ambience of the library, I acquired the diligent habits of fellow students and scholars. The importance of being engrossed in scholarly pursuits was etched upon my mind. Thus, I began to inculcate a habit of voracious reading, exploring various topics and disciplines, advancing my knowledge, and expanding perspectives. With firm determination and persistence, I diligently applied myself to the pursuit of academics.

Through relentless effort and a strong determination to better oneself, I witnessed a dramatic transformation unfolding. Despite the setback, my resilience and determination paid off in incredible measure. Indeed, gaining a score of 9 out of 10 on the test is enough proof of the strength of resilience, coupled with the belief in oneself, to emerge victorious.

When you start to imagine gaining confidence in your mind, it often prompts you into thinking of changing your habits, thus paving the way to the process of acquiring confidence.

Starting the cycle of habit change and emerging victorious, indeed, is profound affirmation of one's ability to have goals and to pursue them to completion. This tangible proof of success is bound to bring about a sense of power within you, thus increasing your confidence in your ability to take charge of your life.

Habit change oftentimes entails the development of self-discipline and the willpower to avoid instant gratification in preference of the long-term benefits. As you embark on these challenges and exercise restraint over your desires, you not only grow your willpower but also grow your confidence in your capability to manage yourself and your behavioral components.

Besides, the acquisition of positive habits tends to be reciprocated by positive results within the arena of life, whether in the aspect of health, productivity, or relationship quality. These tangible evidence of success tend to be powerful reinforcements, which solidize your conviction in your ability to bring about meaningful change and thus contribute to an increased level of self-assurance.

By being in control of your habits and by orchestrating deliberate change, you become the master of your life and empower yourself to make your destiny. Indeed, this newfound sense of empowerment permeates other aspects of your life, and the deep-seated confidence that stems from it permeates all aspects of your being.

Apart from this, as you become committed to the act of habit change and maintain follow-through, you develop a deep level of trust in yourself. This self-trust forms the bedrock on which confidence is built as you learn to trust your own judgment and abilities to lead you through the complexities of life and to deal with life's setbacks.

In other words, habit change is a powerful means for gaining confidence and self-belief. It involves taking a series of small but meaningful steps toward self-improvement, every small victory tending to solidify your personal worth and potential. Through this process of growth and development, you are well-positioned to tap into the fullest of your potential and realize the limitless possibilities that lie within.

If you read a book or any article about how to build confidence, you may come across dozens of points that leave you utterly confused and disappointed by the answers you receive. Here, I shall share with you how I build my confidence.

I come from northern India. I started my professional career as a political consultant, and my first job was to manage a political campaign in Meghalaya.

Meghalaya is a northeastern state in India, known for beautiful landscapes and rich cultural heritage. It is located in the northeast of India, on the border with Assam and Bangladesh. Its capital is Shillong, and it is sometimes referred to as the "Scotland of the East" because of its beautiful scenery. Meghalaya is green in hills and forests, with multiple rivers and waterfalls. Its population consists of different tribes—the Khasis, Garos, and Jaintias—and all speak their own languages and have their traditions. The main languages spoken are Khasi and Garo, but English is also spoken here. Tourists like Meghalaya for places like the living root bridges in Cherrapunji, the super-clean Mawlynnong village, and the Nohkalikai Falls, one of the tallest waterfalls in India. Agriculture, tourism, and mining are its main industries.

Big portions of the economy here, especially since Meghalaya has lots of coal, limestone, and uranium. The weather is usually nice with a mild climate, but it rains a lot during the monsoon season from June to September. Meghalaya is a place of beauty, diversity, and welcoming people, and therefore, a must-see in India.

Two areas were to carry out the campaigns: one was Shillong, and the other was Tura. I was to oversee the campaigns in Tura.

Tura is a city in the Indian state of Meghalaya. Located in the West Garo Hills district, it is a town in the west of the state, near Bangladesh. After Shillong, it is the second largest town in Meghalaya. It lies between the Brahmaputra River, surrounded by lush hills and forests, and that is a picturesque setting.

Tura is known for its rich culture, mainly represented by the Garo people that inhabit the city. Many festivals and events take place here, giving a taste of their culture and traditions. The town is also the commercial center of Meghalaya, with markets over-swarmed with traders. Agriculture is an important activity here, with locals producing crops like rice, maize, and oranges in fertile plains. Tourism is also an important aspect, as the beauty of nature and cultural richness of Tura attracts many visitors. Scenic spots, waterfalls, and Garo villages are some of the most visited sites of Tura. Tura, therefore, forms a perfect blend of nature, culture, and commerce, a very important place in Meghalaya.

The first problem I faced was transportation. Being a very green hills and forest area, the roads are narrow, and in some cases, it can be really frustrating. When you have motion sickness, that place can seem like hell.

Motion sickness, often referred to as nausea or vertigo, is the effect of experiencing nausea or dizziness, or the urge to vomit, while experiencing movement. It is commonly experienced during automobile travel, boat rides, air travel, or riding amusement park rides. Motion sickness causes nausea because of sensations in the inner ear, which aids the body with balance and motion, but the eyes and body don't. This internal mismatching of feelings can cause nausea and dizziness.

I had to travel around 200-300 kilometers per day along the winding roads, and I've got this problem with motion sickness. When I traveled through those winding roads for the first time, I vomited many times during the two hours.

So, I worked on my thought process. I told myself that I would have to go through this difficulty till I felt better. After 6-7 days, I started to overcome my motion sickness.

My first lesson is that if you want to build your confidence, you should start working on your thought process. By creating a positive environment around you, by believing that you can do it and you will do it. You start to develop habits based on your thought process. That leads to increased confidence.

At a very tender age of 16, a famous Indian cricketer found himself in a very challenging situation. He was facing seasoned fast bowlers who, in succession, were bowling a bouncer that hit him on the nose and did so continuously that the whole ground began to resemble a pool with blood all around. The sight was very horrifying to the viewers, who for a moment questioned the fairness of exposing such a small boy to the field of ordeals. The team's medical staff rushed into the ground to save him and recommended the first call of retreat from the ground followed by further treatment and recuperation before returning to the ground. However, in a miraculous act of resilience, the young cricketer shouted, "I will play!" Everyone was enraptured by his inner strength. Instead of retreating to the comfort of the dressing room, he made it to the ground to face the challenges and there himself. That hour was one of great genesis for a budding career and the emergence of a cricketing star of the future.

The 16-year-old player made a positive atmosphere around himself by declaring, "I will play," which brought positive vibes around him. That mentally gave him ample boost to become a star in the cricketing arena.

Creating a positive environment truly helps in boosting confidence.

Yes

One of my friends asked why the method of thinking positively didn't work for him?

I asked him where he was applying this method.

He told me that he gambles and tries to think positively, believing that he will win the game. He thought that by creating a positive environment around him, he would increase his chances of winning.

However, despite his positive mindset, he didn't win the gambling game.

That's a valid question you might ask: why, despite always thinking positively, haven't I gained confidence? The thing is, my friend, is using positive vibrations for his own greed.

If you're also using positive vibes for your greed, it won't help you much. When you create positive vibes, you're trying to connect with the almighty God, seeking help from Him. However, if you apply your positive vibes to your greed, God might not assist you because you're indirectly focusing on greed, which already creates negative vibes. If negative vibes persist, your positive ones won't work effectively.

Here is another example of how creating a positive environment helped me gain confidence.

When I was working as a political consultant, I had the opportunity to closely collaborate with the former chief minister, Meghalaya, spearheading political campaigns for him. However, there was a campaign launched by the company that I felt was not up to par, and it was not yielding the desired results.

So, I approached my manager with an idea. I proposed that if the ex-chief minister himself participated in the campaign registration process, it would inspire other leaders to follow suit, thereby boosting the campaign's effectiveness.

My manager appreciated the idea and suggested discussing it with the director, but I was confident in my approach. I assured him that I would personally convince the ex-chief minister to volunteer for the registration process.

I visited the ex-chief minister and shared my idea with him. He was impressed and agreed to participate as a volunteer for the registration drive. He asked for some time to prepare and then enthusiastically began registering common people as a volunteer just two hours later.

How did I gain enough confidence to convince the ex-chief minister?

I had developed a positive mindset about my idea, with no expectations in return. My sole aim was to assist him in boosting his campaign. This genuine intention resonated with him, leading to his immediate agreement.

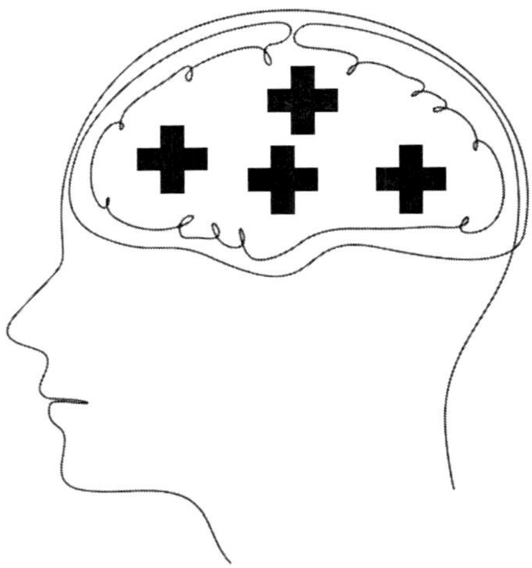

Summary:

- When you start thinking about becoming more confident, it might make you think about changing some of your habits, which can help you become more confident over time.

- The first lesson is that if you want to build your confidence, you should start working on your thought process. Create a positive environment around yourself by believing that you can do it and you will do it. When you begin to think positively, your mind starts developing habits based on your thought process, leading to increased confidence.
- If you're using positive vibes just to get what you want, it won't work out well. When you create positive vibes, you're trying to connect with God and ask for help. But if you're only thinking about getting more for yourself, God might not help because you're focusing on greed, which creates negativity. If there's too much negativity, your positive vibes won't work as well.
- Create positive vibes without any selfishness or expectation, and you'll naturally attract what you desire.

CHAPTER - 4

REALIZATION: SEEK YOURSELF - WHO YOU ARE?

Take a look at this image and try to understand who you truly are.

How will you look for yourself and get the result that you are looking for:

While I was working as a political consultant, my company ran a campaign for the voters of Meghalaya, which was marketed as a financial inclusion program for women's empowerment. Under this scheme, they said they would directly transfer 1000 rupees per month to every woman in every household. So they did a registration program where volunteers visited every household and informed women that they would get 1000 rupees once our party came into power. They were given a card that looked like an ATM card, but no magnetic strip; it was just a symbolic card. When I came to know about the scheme, I immediately expressed my apprehension that it wouldn't work and would only raise doubts among the voters.

How?

Because I analyzed it, I could guess that the scheme would be a total disaster. Sadly, my guesses turned out to be accurate as the party for which my company was working lost to the opposition in a huge manner.

My company was giving a card that looked like an ATM card. When people got a card which looked like an ATM card, people automatically thought that it would give them a lot of benefits on the spot-be it money or coupons. So, people tried to use the card at the ATM, but that card was only a symbolic card that created doubt in the voters' minds.

Secondly, when volunteers visited every household and explained the scheme, promising ₹1000 per month once the party came into power, voters had doubts. They wanted to know how the money would be transferred without giving the bank account numbers.

These were the things I had already analyzed and had been warning my people on the first day of its launch, but alas, nobody listened to me.

How do I analyze?

For any campaign, if you emphasize greed, it's doomed to fail. Unfortunately, that's exactly what my company did. They told everyone that when volunteers went to households, they would introduce our scheme, promising that when our government came into power, every woman in the house would be given 1000 rupees.

That created doubt in the minds of the voters, and they realized that this scheme was a greed-driven one. That's how they rejected it, which amounted to a major defeat for the party.

Reflect on your life, your thinking, and your doings.

If you reflect on your life and feel that you are not getting what you want, then reflect on how many times you have had negative thoughts about others, how often you used bad words, and how many times did greed cloud your prayers.

On the part of employed people, reflect on the time you participated in office politics and how many times you used lies.

In relationships, reflect on the times you have been dishonest or unfaithful, how your ego got in your way, and moments of ill-treatment to your partner.

And for business owners, reflect on the happiness of your employees and whether you have made a happy workplace.

I have witnessed so many tired faces who work in a company.

When I asked them what was troubling them, they said, "they were not at peace."

Do you look like the people who work in a company from 9:30 AM to 8-9 PM and are still not satisfied? You work because you have to pay EMIs, cover your family's expenditures, and live your lifestyle.

When you get a scratch in your body, you feel the pain in your body, which tells you either to get professional medical treatment from a doctor or simply put a bandage on to soothe the pain because you take care of the feeling of physical pain—by going to see a doctor or by doing it yourself.

But what about your mental pain? Ever felt peace of mind? Now close your eyes and try to find yourself—where you are and what you are doing. Is this what you really want? Is this why you work?

I was working in a company, and I found a pattern; till 4 pm, managers and management didn't give out any work. But just when employees started to prepare to leave for home, after 2 hours, the managers started giving them tasks that took too much time to complete, and the employees had to work late into the night. This working culture went on, and these employees were feeling frustrated and started cursing the company and management. So that negative environment led to losing projects for the company.

This is the reason why self-realization becomes necessary for businessmen as well. I have seen many times that managers, for the sake of their own convenience, burden employees with excessive workloads, and even company owners fail to understand why they are making profits. The answer is simple: if you don't ensure your employees' happiness while they work for you, you'll lose profits because they harbor negativity. Therefore, as a businessman, it's critical to realize that apart from business prospects, your profits rely on how your employees perceive and feel about your company.

If you're a student, professional, in a relationship, or a businessman, consider whether what you're doing brings you peace.

It's time to analyze your daily routine: what you do when you wake up, what you consume in the morning, your activities throughout the day, the meals you have eaten, and what you do when you return home. Consider how much time you devote to yourself. One thing to remember is that watching reels or spending time on social media doesn't necessarily mean you're spending time for yourself.

One night, while I was sleeping in my hostel room, I suddenly woke up to a loud noise, which sounded like a thud. When I opened my door, I saw many students moving around outside the corridor. I asked them what had happened and what the noise was.

Someone told me that a student had jumped from the third floor of the hostel and attempted suicide.

I was shocked.

That boy was a third-year student at a premier institute. Getting admission to this institute is not easy, as it requires passing a tough exam. You need to have a bright mind to succeed in the examination and secure admission.

As if to that effect, how could one have thought about committing suicide with an active mind? That was the question everybody was asking.

I heard it was due to pressure to perform so perfectly in class.

I am sharing another experience with you. There was a girl who had always excelled in her academics, consistently ranking as a top performer. She was dedicated to her studies and was currently pursuing her Ph.D., maintaining impeccable academic records.

However, one fateful day, I was shocked to hear the devastating news that she had taken her own life by hanging herself from the ceiling fan.

As I delved deeper into the circumstances surrounding her tragic death, I learned that she was enduring severe mental anguish caused by her husband and his family. They were relentlessly pressuring her for dowry, subjecting her to constant emotional and psychological torment.

Despite her academic prowess and achievements, she found herself ensnared in a situation where her mental well-being was compromised by the insidious demands of her marital relationship. This heartbreaking incident serves as a poignant reminder of the profound impact that societal pressures and familial expectations can have on an individual's mental health and overall sense of well-being.

If you excel in academics and possess a brilliant mind, it doesn't necessarily mean that you have the ability to withstand societal and mental pressures. Many people, despite their intellectual abilities, succumb to the weight of these pressures and tragically resort to suicide.

You will always experience pressure in life. As a student, you'll feel academic and family pressure; as an employee, you'll feel pressure from work and family; as a girl /Women you will feel societal pressure and as a businessman, You'll experience pressure from losses; it's a natural part of life. However, you have the ability to handle these challenges, especially if you know yourself and have recognized your inner strength.

In physics. Pressure is defined as

the force per unit area. Its formula is expressed as

P = F/A,

where P represents pressure, F stands for force, and A denotes the area by which the force is applied perpendicularly.

From the mathematical formula, it is clear that

When the surface area is smaller, the object exerts more pressure. Conversely, when the surface area is larger, the points of contact between the object and the surface increase, resulting in less pressure exerted by the object on the surface.

So, if you want to minimize pressure in your life, expand your perspective, and you can achieve this by connecting with God. When you connect with God, you broaden your mindset and your thoughts, which helps reduce the pressure in your life. When you begin to understand yourself better, you'll find a way to connect with God.

Allocate time for introspection, contemplating your emotions, and evaluating your experiences. Identify sources of happiness, stress triggers, and long-term aspirations. Keep a journal to regularly document your thoughts and emotions to build clarity and self-awareness. Include mindfulness practices such as meditation and deep breathing to calm your mind and intensify your inner being. Notice your reactions in various settings, check their suitability with your beliefs.

Engage in activities that fill you with contentment and joy, trying out new hobbies to understand yourself in more depth.

She was so happy because she was going to marry him. Though it was not a love marriage but an arranged one, she was content because her family members were happy and she wanted to settle down.

Before the marriage, she had a chat over the phone with the groom and gradually developed an emotional attachment with him. She also met his family members and felt they were nice people.

On the first night after the marriage, her mother-in-law came into her room and said that since her father did not provide the dowry, they demanded a car, and since it was not given, she would have to sleep alone until they received the dowry.

She came to know that the people, whom she thought were kind-hearted, were actually greedy. She looked into the eyes of the groom, hoping he, being educated, would say something against his mother. However, the groom made no protest and left the room with his mother.She spent her first night alone, thinking about what was going on in her life and the will of God. It was like watching a movie.

The groom's family started harassing her for dowry. Every morning, her mother-in-law started cursing her father, and the whole evening until night.

She felt frustrated and called her mother and told her the situation. Her mother told her that things would be fine with time. But things never got better. Every day, she used to stay alone whereas her husband used to stay in another room.

She went back to her father's house and started living with her parents. One day, she received a court notice accusing her of running away from her husband's house and stealing the jewelry.

She was again surprised at what was happening to her. She responded to the notice and asked for divorce, but her husband refused to give it. On the date of the court, he submitted an application for not being able to attend the court proceedings, and the procedure is still going on.

But during this period, she was very depressed and had suicidal thoughts in her mind. However, her family members supported her and helped her out. She started self-realization to understand why this was happening to her. She went to a spiritual organization where she lived for nearly 15 days. There, she woke up early in the morning, kept aside her mobile phone, meditated, carried out Yagya, and felt peace in her mind.

She indirectly created positive vibrations by doing so, and now the stage of self-realization was complete. She aligned her vibrations with God. She left her parents' house and started searching for a job, and after some time, she found one. Today, she is working, earning money, and is independent. She knows how to handle difficulties.

She thought during those bad times why this was happening only to her. But after self-realization and connecting with God, she confessed that whatever happened to her was ultimately good for her. If those things had not happened, she would not have become an independent girl, learned how to handle difficulties, or discovered her inner strength.

How do you know when it's time for self-realization?

You can know when it is time for the realization of self when you get inner turmoil or dissatisfaction with the particular life you are leading, or when you start to question beliefs, values, and purpose. Signs may be an experience of being lost, disconnected, or unfulfilled, and also awareness of patterns of behavior or thought that hamper the growth of the individual. Such realization comes from a drive for development in person and the drive to know oneself. This is an internal process that differs from one individual to another.

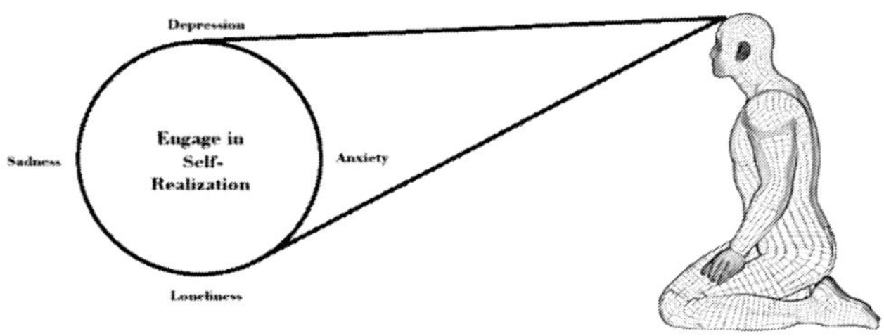

If you are a student, you may not feel good during your academics; studying may bring feelings of sadness.

As a worker or employee, you might experience sadness and depression while working, feeling as though life is a burden and experiencing anxiety.

You may also feel dissatisfied with your relationships and interactions with relatives.

These are indicators that you may need some self-relaxation.

Take two or three days off, start meditating, and empty your mind completely. Begin to think that God is giving you direction and showing you the path that is most suitable for you.

You are the most powerful Soul-

It is there within you; feel its force, feel your energy pulsing deep within. You can do all you want. But at times, you may not realize this power within you, despite the ability to change your life.

In one of the greatest Hindu epics, Ramayana, there's a tale of Hanuman, an extraordinary god of strength and devotion to Lord Rama, who would accompany him on his quest to find his wife, Sita, who has been kidnapped by the demon king Ravana. Through their quest, they had to cross many challenges and obstacles. They needed to cover the vast ocean from their native Lanka because Sita was held there by the villainous king Ravana.

For such a quest, they needed to jump over the ocean. To accomplish this, Hanuman is reminded of his extraordinary ability to fly: a God-given power bestowed upon him.

In a moment of doubt and forgetfulness, Hanuman started to question his own powers. "Is it possible I will successfully jump across the ocean? Is it possible for me to jump across the ocean in search of Sita?" As he was plagued by these questions, Hanuman, who was to fly over the ocean, forgot about his divine capabilities and became powerless.

Jamvant reminded Hanuman of his power through his words of praise and reminder of his extraordinary deeds and the divine origins of Hanuman, the son of the wind god Vayu. He reminded Hanuman of his jumping from the mountains to the ocean in search of Sita and of his invincible strength in all battles against the powerful demons. He told Hanuman of his divine lineage and asked him to remember his true potential as a powerful warrior and devoted servant of Lord

Rama. Through these encouraging words and praise, Jamvant replaced Hanuman's confusion and lack of faith in his abilities with renewed confidence and determination, so that he could fulfill his sacred duty.

It is only when he is reminded of his true nature and the purpose of his mission, to rescue Sita and serve Lord Rama, that Hanuman's faith is restored. With a renewed

Over the vast ocean, with eyes closed and arms lifted in prayer, Hanuman leaps with all his might to reach Lanka's island.

It teaches us an important lesson about faith, courage, and believing in ourselves. Sometimes, the weakest persons lose their power due to doubt and uncertainty. But reconnecting with oneself and staying true to the purpose could always make it possible to overcome any obstacle and achieve the impossible.

Let's do some exercise.

Read this aloud again: "I am the strongest soul in the world, I am mighty, I am successful, I am an unstoppable force of nature, I can pass any interview with ease, I can accomplish anything. I am very confident and can manage all the difficulties in my life with ease.

As you speak these words, pay attention to whether you feel a surge of energy flowing within you. This means you are tapping into your inner strength and reminding yourself of the things that you can do.

When you wake up in the morning, affirm to yourself that you are the most powerful soul, capable of achieving anything you desire. Remind yourself that you are the best and that you have the strength to overcome any obstacle.

Summary:

- Self-realization will bring you peace.
- No matter how educated you are, if you don't seek yourself, you won't find peace.
- Empty your mind completely, close your eyes, and ask God to give you direction that is suitable for you.

CHAPTER - 5

GRATITUDE

When you express gratitude to the universe or anyone else, it fosters a positive environment around you, causing circumstances that may have been working against you to turn positive, thereby helping you overcome your problems.

Gratitude is a tool to create a positive environment.

This is an incredibly powerful feeling that actually changes our lives altogether. Gratitude is the state of feeling thankful and appreciative for whatever good things are in our lives. When we focus on being grateful, we truly will tune in to the highest-positive-radio-station, and that will bring even more good things our way.

In this chapter, we will dive into gratitude, its effects on our moods, and how science unravels it, easy ways to inject more gratitude into our daily lives, and how that makes us feel better and healthier.

Gratitude is like a special kind of energy. It is connected with positive feelings like happiness and love. According to scientists, everything in the universe is made up of energy that is vibrating at different frequencies. Thoughts and feelings send energy waves that mix with the energy in the environment around us. Gratitude sends out a super high-energy vibe that's similar to what love and happiness do.

Let's take an example-

Take, for instance, a head massager, a simple yet illustrative tool composed of numerous wires, each varying in size. As you engage one wire by setting it into motion, either through manual manipulation or an external force, you'll observe a fascinating phenomenon unfold: the adjacent wires of similar length will begin to vibrate in tandem. This occurrence underscores a principle akin to resonance, wherein the energy from the initially activated wire is transferred to its neighboring counterparts, causing them to oscillate harmoniously. Such a demonstration not only elucidates the concept of vibrational synchronization but also serves as a metaphor for the interconnectedness and mutual influence pervasive in various aspects of our lives.

That means you will create positive vibrations when you express gratitude, and in return, you will receive positivity. That is why it is advisable to start a day by expressing gratitude to all the people you can, setting a positive tone for the rest of the day.

The importance of gratitude in our physical and mental well-being can be seen from research.

Research clearly shows the role of gratitude in our physical and mental well-being. Studies have shown that gratitude can improve mood, increase happiness levels, decrease stress, and improve overall psychological health. Such thoughts towards blessings in our lives and cherishing what we have thus shift our energies towards positivity and attract more positive experiences.

Amidst the swirling and bustling rhythm of our lives, it becomes increasingly vital to purposefully slow down and fit in mindfulness to make space for much room in which a deep appreciation for life can thrive within our hearts and minds, simply by pausing, taking a deep breath, and fully immersing ourselves in what's around us, thus opening awareness to the little intricacies that are so often missed and leading to the increased sense of mindfulness within us as we learn to truly appreciate the innate beauty and the richness of our current circumstances while at the same time acknowledging and embracing the many blessings that come to surround us in their gentle embrace.

A gratitude journal is a very powerful tool to cultivate gratitude and raise your vibrational frequency. Take just a few minutes each day to write down the things you are grateful for. This may sound simple, but it can be anything from a beautiful sunset, a loving gesture by a friend, or a delicious meal. By intentionally acknowledging and appreciating the good in our lives, we are training our minds to focus on gratitude and attract even more positivity into our lives.

Gratitude is not just being thankful for good things; it also involves finding something good in bad times. When we are able to reframe our problems in our minds into an opportunity for growth, we can feel thankful even when things get a little rough. When we reframe how we see problems and view them as opportunities to grow, we can feel thankful even in hard times. This helps us notice the hidden blessings and feel more joy on average.

Thanking others strengthens our bonds, but it also makes us feel more thankful. So, take a moment to thank people who have touched your life. Maybe it's through a note or a call or even a simple "Thanks." When we thank others, it creates good vibes and makes our bonds even better.

Gratitude provides us with a magnetic pull toward positive things. It's almost as if there is a law of physics, stating that a good feeling attracts more good feelings. So, being grateful, we tend to pull even more good stuff into our lives: new opportunities, good things happening, and so on. By acknowledging what we already have, we are, in a nutshell, inviting the universe to bring us even more good stuff.

The expression of gratitude not only improves the quality of our existing relationships but also creates much deeper connections with our surrounding environment. When we thank our family, friends, and colleagues at work, we create positive connections and positive exchanges of energy. Gratitude fuels the fire of appreciation, sympathy, and understanding so that deeper and more meaningful connections can be created.

The practice of gratitude makes us more tuned to the vibrational field of happiness and joy. As we cultivate appreciation, we connect with the endless well of happiness inside of us, feeling a great sense of contentment and satisfaction. Gratitude takes us from scarcity to abundance. In doing this, we will appreciate what is going on in our lives and the simple pleasures in life.

Gratitude and appreciation are some of the most potent and powerful words in the English language. Unfortunately, many people tend to take this precious gift of life for granted and fail to see that it is the most precious thing one can have. Therefore, we should celebrate this experience of life, embracing it instead of feeding fear into the fear of what we don't know.

You can turn your whole day and life around just by immersing yourself in the emotion and the vibration of gratitude.

Consider your path, from where you were to where you are today, respecting each step and experience. Acknowledge how Life has been with you and guiding you forward.

Seeing the magnificent placing and timing of events, even those you struggled with, inspire you to wonder with overflowing hearts.

Witnessing the Universe organizing and connecting energy is always at your back to support your focus—a huge happiness and appreciation.

We place a fresh apple with a rotten apple:

Case-1 The fresh apple is more likely to start decaying faster

Case-2 Rotten fruits are more likely to start flourishing faster.

Obviously, Case-1 will happen because rotten fruits emit ethylene gas, which accelerates the ripening and decay of nearby fruits, including other apples. So, it's improbable that both apples would get fresher; instead, the fresh apple might deteriorate more rapidly due to the influence of the rotting one.

Yes, that's correct. The release of ethylene gas by the rotting apple is a natural process that accelerates the decay of nearby fruits, including the fresh apple. Similarly, in various contexts, negativity can indeed have a swift and potent impact on its surroundings. Just as ethylene gas speeds up the decay of the fresh apple, negative influences can quickly affect the environment, highlighting the importance of fostering positivity and resilience to counteract such effects.

However, when we are angry at someone, it is all too tempting to curse them or make fun of them. However, we should understand that indulging in such behavior will inadvertently attract negative energy to ourselves. Such negative energy may then have negative impacts on us, both mentally and physically. Though it may seem impractical or even counterintuitive to think positively of someone who has hurt us, it is crucial to understand the enormity of the effects that holding on to negative thoughts towards him can bring onto our own lives. In fact, feeding on bitterness, resentment, or animosity towards those who have wronged us often serves as a self-inflicted wound—an injury that festers and bleeds negativity into our own minds and hearts.

When we wallow ourselves in anger or hostility towards another, we in turn expose ourselves to a constant whirlwind of emotional distress and psychological turmoil. Our thoughts are consumed by feelings of bitterness, replaying past grievances and inventing scenarios of retribution. In the process, we unknowingly surrender our own peace of mind to the very people who have hurt us.

Moreover, negative emotions are not just mentally torturing but seep into all facets of life, corrupting and souring overall well-being. Long-term exposure to negative emotions is known to lead to a number of negative physical and psychological consequences: increased stress levels, weakened immune systems, and an increased likelihood of developing mental health diseases such as depression and anxiety.

Such outcomes only indicate the detrimental consequences that this antagonistic attitude toward others cannot lead us to. What is needed is the creation of a positive milieu both inside and outside our circle, the choice to focus on the present, to embrace forgiveness and compassion, and to channel our energy toward works that support our growth and well-being.

This allows the orientation to be positive and resilient. It empowers ourselves to go beyond the grievances of the past and to chart a course for healing and renewal. Instead of becoming victims of others' actions, it reclaims agency for ourselves in order to take our lives to a brighter and more fulfilling future. In this manner, we not only free ourselves from resentment but we also inspire others to do the same.

It is spreading positivity and kindness and, in turn, creating ripples that go beyond our individual lives.

Let me tell you a story about Gautama Buddha and this horrible thug, Angulimala. Angulimala was a criminal known for his ferocity and terror because he wore a necklace from his murdered victims. However, even with such a man so dangerous in his presence, Gautama Buddha met Angulimala with compassion and understanding.

Instead of renouncing Angulimala for his evil deeds in the past, Gautama Buddha saw within this man a chance to live in good. Patiently, he led Angulimala through his psyche and his past toward redemption.

With Gautama Buddha's teachings and guidance, Angulimala experienced a change within himself. He stopped being a terrorist and a torturer and joined the ranks of honorable monks in the Buddhist world.

By this story, we learn the power of love and forgiveness. Instead of getting angry or seeking revenge, Gautama Buddha showed empathy and forgiveness, finally leading Angulimala to spiritual enlightenment. It proves that love and forgiveness indeed are powerful forces for making the world better.

compassion to heal even the deepest wounds and bring about profound transformation in the hearts of individuals.

How to create the positive environment?

If you want to create a positive environment around you, refrain from thinking negatively about anyone. Often, people claim they are thinking positively, but indirectly, they attract negative vibrations. For instance, commenting that today's food was not good is inviting negative vibrations. If you attract negative vibrations, whether directly or indirectly, it becomes challenging to foster positive ones.

A person claimed to be practicing positive affirmations but wasn't seeing positive results. When I asked him how many people he had told about it, he mentioned only me and a few others. I pointed out that by stating that positive affirmations weren't working for him, he was attracting negative vibrations. Instead of saying that positive affirmations weren't effective, he should have expressed gratitude to God for creating positivity in his mind. After some days, things started working out for him.

How to express your gratitude to God?

"I thank You, God, for bequeathing me the priceless treasure of human life, for accompanying me with everlasting love and for fulfilling all my needs, as well as for success and confidence in myself, for Your heavenly direction light my path, for the blessings of wealth and prosperity You shower on me, for the glorious beauty You adorn my life, and for ever guiding my steps to what is right.

Thank you, dear Lord, for all the blessings in my life. You've given me more than I could have ever wished. For loving family and friends to look out for me and keep me in their hearts. Every day, they help me through life by loving me and letting the glow of the goodness you have shown shine within me, keeping me on my knees toward you.

Thank you for keeping me safe and helping me to keep the right choices. You provide me wise guides to walk through life's tough times and I always have your guidance, letting me know that you are always there with me during the darkest of times.

Thank you for watching over my loved ones, too. Help me demonstrate to them every day how much they mean to me, and give me the strength to treat them with the same kindness they have shown me.

Summary:

- Recognize the signs from God.
- When you're in trouble and no one's there to help, it's a sign to connect with God.
- Once you connect with God, you'll feel peace, and He'll guide you on your life path.
- Express Your Gratitude to God.

CHAPTER - 6

GOD WILL CALL YOU WHEN NEEDED

Many times, we dismiss the existence of God, considering the concept merely as imagination and believing that God doesn't exist. We often cite scientific facts to support the notion that God is non-existent.

But when you engage in deep introspection, you will find that Albert Einstein later presented the concept of energy and mass, whereas in the spiritual realm, the concept of body and soul had already been elucidated.

In today's world, we are connected through the body. If we have to communicate with someone, we use our physical bodies, such as mobile phones, through which we can hear sound waves and converse. However, in the spiritual realm, people communicate through energy, so they don't require physical bodies. Unfortunately, we often fail to grasp this concept because we are not accustomed to utilizing energy for communication.

But just how powerful is energy? To understand its magnitude, consider the concept of the atom bomb. In an atom bomb, mass is converted into energy, yielding an immense power capable of destroying the world.

In today's technical world, we are focused on the material aspects. We perform operations using equipment and physical instruments, such as mobile phones and computers, to transmit waves from one place to another. Consequently, many people struggle to grasp the concept of energy and supreme energy.

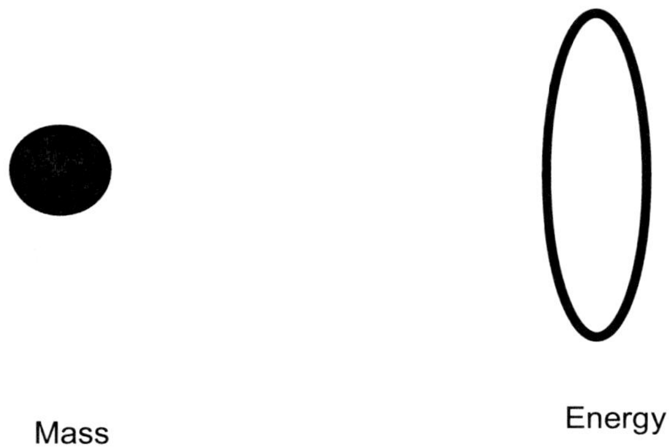

This is another common experience of people in this world: they seem to forget about energy and the existence of a Supreme Energy Source, and this is commonly known as God. But when they are in trouble or when they find themselves in a desperate situation with no one—no family, no parents, or no impersonal systems around them—then they begin to call out for energy and a higher power, in fact, God.

When life serves you a lemon, hey, it's actually a call from God. He is nudging you to make your vibe ring with His.

Have you ever heard the story about Prahlad? He was a prince in ancient India and a very devout boy who believed in Lord Vishnu. He refused to worship his father, the mighty demon king Hiranyakashipu. Despite the fact that he endured his father's torture and punishment, Prahlad never lost his mind and never betrayed Lord Vishnu. He believed steadfastly that God was omnipresent and relied on the power of God's protection.

When Hiranyakashipu, once again, tried to break Prahlad's belief, he had challenged Prahlad to prove whether Vishnu really existed. He was confident that if Vishnu did exist, he would surely save Prahlad. Prahlad was undaunted; he stood calm and strong. As Hiranyakashipu launched his attack, Lord Vishnu appeared as Narasimha, the well-known half-man, half-lion avatar, who defeated Hiranyakashipu and saved Prahlad. This epic story of Prahlad is a shining example of how one's unrelenting belief and devotion have an almighty power because Prahlad was not only undaunted but had impressed one and all by his resilience and strength in the face of adversity.

Recognize God's

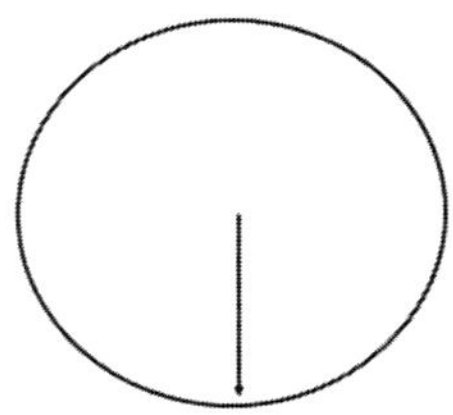

When your life is going smoothly and you have no problems, it may mean that there are no signals from God.

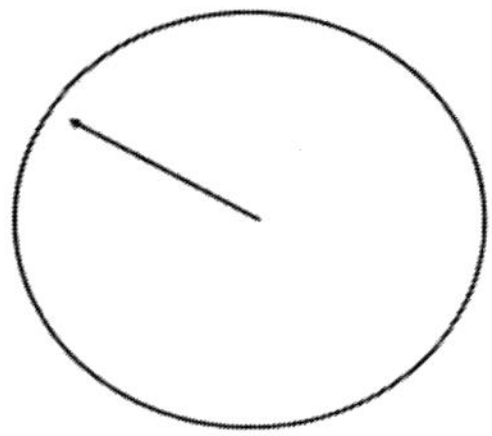

When you face difficulties and find no one to help you, it's time to recognize God's signal.

How do I recognize the signal of God?

In the office where I was working, they started firing people without any proper reason and at that time, witnessing the worried expressions on people's faces, knowing that they might be terminated the next day, filled me with sadness. The company's conduct had cultivated a negative atmosphere, discouraging employees from working with passion and dedication. Seeing the negativity, I resigned from my job. I always try to escape from negative energy; however, my company did not accept my resignation letter.

During that period when the company was conducting layoffs, they held several meetings to retain my services because as an employee, I consistently performed my work with passion and honesty. They offered me a salary hike, and my manager took my laptop and wrote an email to revoke my resignation.

However, many people were okay with working in that negative environment because of a lack of opportunities.

Though that may have been God's wish, so I started working again. However, after one month, they started firing people again, and they did not give me the promised dues. So, I wrote an email to the director stating that I am launching a Non-Cooperation Movement following the ideology of Gandhi Ji, and I left. My company again emailed me to come back, but they did not clear my dues. So, I questioned why they were not giving me my dues because I had worked hard there.

Not only I, but many employees left that company because of the negative environment.

During this period, I observed that the company was losing its reputation and missing out on business opportunities. I made efforts to communicate this concern, but the company overlooked it, resulting in the loss of several clients. Meanwhile, amidst these events, my friend's former partner began sharing photos of us on social media along with false statements.

In this phase, I came to know why it was happening to me. Initially, I was very frustrated and depressed. Wherever I looked for a helping hand, no one was there to help me. So I started visiting temples and spiritual places, started meditating, and found that I was feeling peaceful. I realized that God was helping me, giving me strength to become stronger, so that I could do something different.

I realized that this difficulty is happening to me because God has another plan for me. God wants to connect with me and do something that I enjoy. He gave me strength, and I started reflecting on what I have done so far and what I want to do. I realized that I am very good at writing, and many times I thought I should pursue my passion for writing, but I did not. So with inspiration from God, I started writing a book so that what I have learned can be helpful to others.

Do you know the story of Muniba Mazari, a motivational speaker? She said that God has a greater plan for you. She said problems are not too big but we are too small, we can't handle it.

Muniba Mazari is an inspiring woman from Pakistan. She faced a life-changing event when she was involved in a car accident at the age of 21. The accident left her paralyzed from the waist down, confining her to a wheelchair. Despite this immense challenge, Muniba didn't lose hope.

She was traveling from Balochistan to her home when the driver fell asleep, and the car came down into a ditch. The accident had left her with multiple injuries; a fractured right arm, shoulder, and collarbone, severe damage to her lungs, liver, and rib cage, and the most life-altering injury was to her spinal cord, where three vertebrae were completely crushed.

She couldn't find an ambulance and, after waiting for more than one hour, she was wheeled into the hospital in the back of a Potohar Jeep. She was totally immobile as half of her body was fractured, and the other half was paralyzed. Unfortunately, the first hospital that she reached dismissed her on grounds that there was no equipment, and that she wouldn't survive. She found refuge in another hospital where she was rejected because doctors refused to operate on her on the grounds that there was no equipment. Finally, she found refuge at the Comparative Burn Unit Hospital in Karachi, where she was admitted.

She was then loaded into an ambulance that took her to the hospital. That hospital was her hope for survival. She remained there for two and a half months. She went through three major and two minor surgeries. She was fitted with many metals in her body, and for this reason, she felt like an iron lady. This stay in the hospital was very challenging for her. She went through immense physical and emotional pain and many people who were going to help her along the way all left on those moments when she needed them most. She felt as if her life was meaningless and boring. She was surrounded by white walls and felt like she was trapped in her suffering. She reached breaking-up time. She would have liked to dwell on those who left her on the wayside or on the fact that her legs did not function anymore, but she had people who cared and much to be thankful for. And so, she decided to stop crying and griping because it did not help.

The best decision she took during this trying time was to start painting. Even with her hand that looked like a deformed piece of wood, she used it to give color to her colorless life. Painting became her recourse and her essence. It kept her alive, amidst her suffering. She was then shifted to Islamabad, where she was bedridden for two years because of multiple pressure ulcers and infections.

Now, after two years and two and a half months of bed rest, doing nothing, the only thing that kept her going was art. Art is such a beautiful medium through which you can express yourself without uttering a single word. But the day she first used a wheelchair, she became a different person. She remembers looking at herself in the mirror and telling herself that she couldn't wait for a miracle to make her walk again, nor could she afford expensive treatments. She couldn't sit in a corner crying and begging for mercy because people didn't have time. So, she decided to accept herself as she was, sooner rather than later.

She wanted to become financially strong and stable, so she began looking for jobs. A good friend of hers found a job posting for a content writer on Facebook. She commented, "Wish I could," and was called for an interview. She got the job, marking the start of her professional career. As she became financially stable, she continued to exhibit her artwork in different galleries, flourishing as an artist. Life was comfortable, but she wasn't content because she always aimed high and thought big. She didn't know how she would achieve her dreams, but she knew she wanted to do something significant for her country and its people.

One day, she watched a campaign advert on polio in which a boy from a poor family sat in a wheelchair crying with his father and begged all the parents to vaccinate their children against polio. Her heart was broken. She was ashamed because the media used a person who is in a wheelchair as a picture of sorrow, misery, and death. This wrong picture of people who are in a wheelchair motivated her to change the picture of people who are in a wheelchair from the public's eyes.

Muniba Mazari has been awarded in many fields, including art, activism, hosting, modelling, singing, and motivational speaking. Even though she has tried a few things, her paints and speaking as a motivator have been her primary focus points.

Definitely, God always has another plan for us, and difficulties often are signs that He is trying to communicate with us. Through these challenges, God adds strength to us so that our positive vibrations can inspire and elevate the hearts of others. Today, Muniba Mazari is a motivational speaker whose story has inspired millions of people's hearts with confidence, motivation, and strength.

Summary:

- God will call upon you when needed.
- If you find yourself in a situation where no one is there to help, take it as a sign that God wants to connect with you.
- He has chosen you so that he can give you a direction suitable for you.

CHAPTER-7

COMPLETE SURRENDER

Surrender usually brings to mind giving up or losing in a fight. But when we surrender to God, it means we're choosing to let go of struggling alone with all the challenges life throws at us, whether they're from the outside world or from within ourselves.

True surrender occurs when we have full trust in God. At that point, God handles all our problems and difficulties, freeing us from suffering.

It's preeminently that we must give our souls to God and have total faith in God. We need to believe that God is and that God organizes everything around us.

Once this belief is firm, the next step is to recognize His will in all that happens. We must understand that everything He does is for our benefit. Just like a child would blindly trust its parents, we must place a blind trust in God totally, knowing well that He knows what is for our good.

After accepting His will, we reach a stage where we surrender our entire being to Him. This means offering our joys, sorrows, and actions to Him. Every aspect of our life becomes dedicated to serving Him, and we trust Him to take care of us.

The final stage of surrender is when we perceive His presence in everything and everyone. We feel connected to Him in all of creation, experiencing oneness with Him.

Often, we may not accept or understand this, but there comes a time when we find ourselves completely alone, with no one to help us – neither our family nor our friends. It is during such situations that we begin to remember God and attempt to surrender ourselves before Him.

> If you find yourself completely alone, with neither your family nor your friends helping you, surrender yourself before God. Speak with Him, share your problems, and seek solace in His presence.

When Dushasana pulled Draupadi's saree at her pleadings before the elders were to be not one but five times. None stepped in to protect her. She implored each of her five husbands: Yudhistara, Arjuna, Bheema, Nakula, and Sahadeva. But all had been made to play the game of dice, which brought them under the control of the Kauravas. In ancient India, women were generally believed to be protected by their husbands. Here was Draupadi with five husbands, but none of them could come to rescue her from disgrace. Clutching at her saree, Draupadi did her best to maintain the sanctity of her body. But Dushasana was not to be deterred. He mercilessly pulled at the saree, causing Draupadi to scream for the help of her God.

Observing Bheem, Draupadi envisioned, "Gadhadhari Bheem will come and shatter his skull." Consequently, Bheemsen bowed his head.

Observing Arjuna, she exclaimed, "Gandivdhari Arjuna will come and smash his teeth!" Consequently, Arjuna, too, bowed his head. Subsequently, one by one, they all bowed their heads due to their loss in the dice game, causing Draupadi to lose faith in them.

Turning to the Dharmacharyas present, including Bhisma, Vidur, Kripacharya, and Dronacharya, she sought their assistance, but once more, she was left disillusioned. Thus, she relied on her own strength and resolve.

When she found herself hopeless and with nobody to help her, she surrendered herself completely in front of Lord Krishna.

In her desperation, Draupadi invoked Krishna as the indweller of her heart, 'Atmanivasi Krishna'. Miraculously, as she uttered these words, her saree began to extend endlessly. Each layer Dushasana pulled off revealed another layer underneath, until he collapsed from exhaustion. Draupadi, with folded hands and closed eyes, continued to chant the name of her savior, Krishna.

Until she turned to God, Draupadi had relied on her own strength and the assistance of others. But it was only when she addressed Krishna as the indweller of her heart that He came to her aid. At that moment, she released her grip on her saree and surrendered herself entirely to Krishna.

This incident teaches us the importance of complete surrender to God. When Draupadi stopped fixating on her attire and body and focused solely on God, He intervened. This exemplifies the essence of surrender—placing unwavering trust in the divine. The lesson is clear: whenever faced with adversity, instead of dwelling on the problem, concentrate on God. He will invariably provide a solution. No matter how daunting the challenge may seem, it is never beyond the scope of God's power.

There the story is:

Once, I was faced with a dilemma of the worst kind as I settled down to fill out a very critical form with the deadline of the following day. This form required either the submission of my grades or the signature of the head of department, but I was in a tight spot because I did not have my results. My university was located a formidable 800 kilometers away and seemed like an insurmountable distance to cover, especially given the fact that it would mean such a trek that would consume over 12 hours of my precious time. Moreover, the possibility of getting the head of department to sign amidst such logistical difficulties appeared uncertain and hard. In such a compelling situation, desperate feelings flooded my heart, and with tears watering my eyes, I humbly submitted to the providence of God, with a heartfelt prayer at the same time acknowledging Him as my sole ray of hope amidst the stormy uncertainty.

In the game of life, so complex and ever-unfolding as a vast and intricate chessboard, the surrender of one player forces one's mind to contemplate whether the human agent, whether of fate or destiny or by a higher power, will play the chessboard of one's destiny with the grace and knowledge of a master play. In a surrender, when I gave up control and trusted in the divine providence of God, a divine intervention took place. As if a master chess player made the move so unexpectedly, God took charge of my affairs, playing events like a sorcerer to amaze all and sundry. And then, in a happy coincidence of fate, as if all the pieces of the puzzle fell into place, the long-awaited result, shrouded in uncertainty until that moment, suddenly appeared on the evening itself, lighting the path forward with new clarity and purpose.

There was a girl who did not believe in God; she had a technical mindset. Once, she found herself seriously ill in a strange town, hospitalized, while her job back home was terminated due to the critical need for a fully staffed team. She spent six weeks in the hospital and faced another six months before she could resume work. With no religious upbringing and uncertain about the existence of God, she was discharged from the hospital with her belongings in storage, facing homelessness and financial uncertainty. Having nowhere to go and just 5000 INR to her name, her car was on the brink of repossession. She was a stranger in the town where she had been hospitalized, with no family or support network.

In desperation, she uttered a prayer, acknowledging the possibility of God's existence and expressing her willingness to seek help. She articulated five urgent needs: companionship, a home base, shelter and sustenance, financial support, and the retention of her car, recognizing them as seemingly insurmountable challenges. She challenged God to intervene, promising to believe and follow him if these needs were met, even though she had no understanding of complete surrender in front of God, yet indirectly she did.

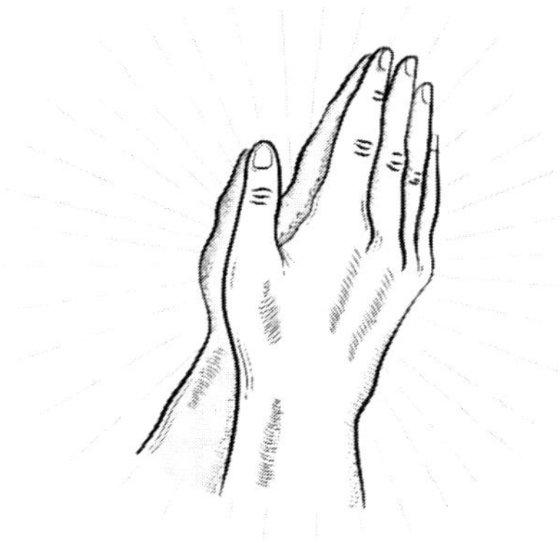

Remarkably, by the next Monday afternoon, all five of her needs had been miraculously fulfilled starting with a surprising encounter with a nurse, who was more than willing to offer her support and invited her into her own home. Support from unexpected sources then followed, defying all probability of natural causes. She was welcomed into a household of caring people who offered her a safe haven until she recovered and got herself a new job. Furthermore, a chance encounter with a bank president led to a loan for her car, even though she was unemployed at the time.

She has faithfully followed God for the past five decades, embracing His teachings and the weight of full submission in her life. She has had countless miracles, including healings and interventions that defy rational explanation. She has learned to appreciate what it means to have unwavering faith and commitment to God, assenting to His supremacy and to the way His Spirit can bring about transformational power in one's life. Her life is a testimony of the reality of God's existence and that, if one places his trust in Him and completely surrenders before GOD, He will be there.

> If no one is there to help you, surrender yourself completely in front of God; He has given you this life, and He will take care of you. While surrendering, have faith in the existence of God, and you will experience miracles.

God- In my divine wisdom, I have chosen you to take birth among all creatures in the form of a human being. I have bestowed upon you the remarkable gift of a three-pound organ known as a brain. With this extraordinary gift, you possess the ability to showcase your intelligence, exert control over your bodily movements, and even engage in the extraordinary feat of prediction. Embrace this divine endowment and use it to navigate the intricate journey of your human existence

Thank You God

In the intricate design of human existence, God pondered on enhancing the tapestry of life, seeking to infuse it with greater intrigue. As a result of divine contemplation, a unique sense was meticulously embedded in our brains — a sense that would come to be known as confusion. This deliberate inclusion was intended to add depth to our experiences, fostering resilience, learning, and the perpetual journey of self-discovery within the intricate dance of life.

Summary:

- God is the mastermind and supreme Soul you can not challenge God.
- Show your gratitude toward the Mastermind and let him play the life game as he wants.
- If you ever find yourself in a situation where you're uncertain of what to do, simply surrender to the Mastermind.
- Express gratitude towards the Mastermind, saying thank you, God, for granting me a good life, thank you God, for blessing me with a human birth, and thank you, God, for providing me with opportunities.
- Thank you, God, even for presenting me with this challenging situation, as it allows me to perceive life from a different perspective.

Trust me, the Mastermind will guide you towards achieving your goals.

CHAPTER - 8

THE GIFT

Gift this book to your friends and family and make them read this chapter especially why?

Think of a time that you received a gift from someone. Remember how you felt? All warm and happy, just like the sun kissing your skin.

More than enjoying a delicious meal, there's some really cool research saying that giving gifts does make us feel good. When you give or receive a gift, those places light up with happiness in your brain. It's like your brain saying, "Hey, this feels really nice!" In addition, there is a chemical known as dopamine, released to help further make you feel happy.

Hence, your parents, friends, and family members must read this chapter because it is all about understanding how positive vibes can make a big difference in our lives.

A helpful hint for parents is that you should not try to compare your child with others as it will bring in negative vibes, which is what we do not want. Instead, let us concentrate on spreading positivity to everyone we know.

Many parents compare their children with others or with their friends' children, noticing that their friend's son has a stable job while their own child works in the private sector. They observe that their friend's child has achieved success while theirs is still striving for it, they share the link or message on WhatsApp or social media, talking about someone's success. They may be trying to motivate their child or dreaming of their child's success, but the approach is always wrong.

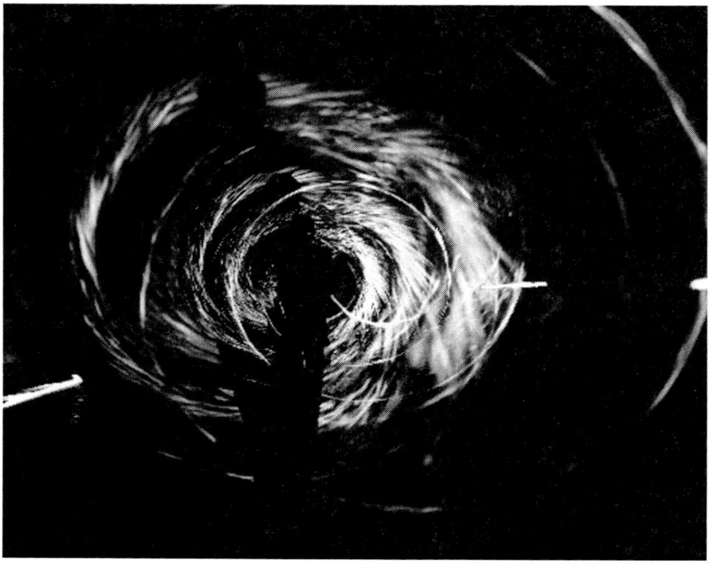

Being a parent, have you ever thought that when you continuously send someone's success story to your children, they are irritated because they are thinking you are comparing them with your friend's children, developing negative vibrations in their mind. The negativity around them makes them not reach the success they desire. Even though your children are working hard and trying their best, they may not achieve the success they desire.

Just try this for 30 days and see the difference.

Call your children and let them know how they are so special and how everything is going on for them, and how God has unique plans for them. Keep a positive environment around them, and you will see the changes in your children's lives. Just do it without criticizing your children, your relatives or anyone else.

Give positive vibrations to your children.

If you are the type of person who has friends who always gossip about others, it is best to avoid that kind of person. Their negative conversations create negative vibes, and if you are resonating with that, you also become the same frequency, and then negative vibes begin to attract towards you, and you start facing problems in your life.

Have you realized that when a person is faced with problems or difficulties in life, they always head to organizations in which they meditate? In such organizations, the first thing they do away with is your mobile phone because in this technologically modern world, mobile phones are the primary medium of receiving negative vibrations.

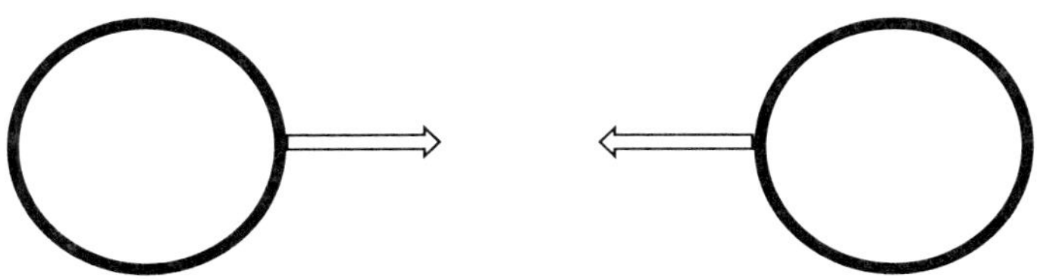

Action **Re-action**

Newton's third law states that every action has an equal and opposite reaction. If you are consuming food and before eating, you send positive thoughts to the food, while eating, you will receive the same energy.

Before consuming the food, say "Thank you, sweet food that I am about to take. You are going to create positive vibes inside me, you are going to create tremendous positive energy inside me. Thank you, food."

Then you will experience the flow of energy inside your body while eating that food because you gave your positive thoughts to food. So, the food will reciprocate with the same positive energy.

Gift positive thoughts to everyone to receive the same in return

Take a glass of water and observe it with positive thoughts. See the water's stability and offer it a positive gift by saying, 'Thank you, water, for giving me stability. Thank you for giving me purity in my mind like you. Thank you for giving me strength like you. You are the greatest source of energy and have provided me with the opportunities I am seeking.' Now, drink slowly and feel the purity. While drinking, affirm that you are pure now, and you will feel a flow of energy inside you.

Summary:

- Gift positivity to your children.
- Gift positive vibrations to the universe.
- Gift your gratitude to your belongings.

Whole Summary:

Life can be compared to a sine graph, where the x-axis represents our age and the y-axis represents our situation.

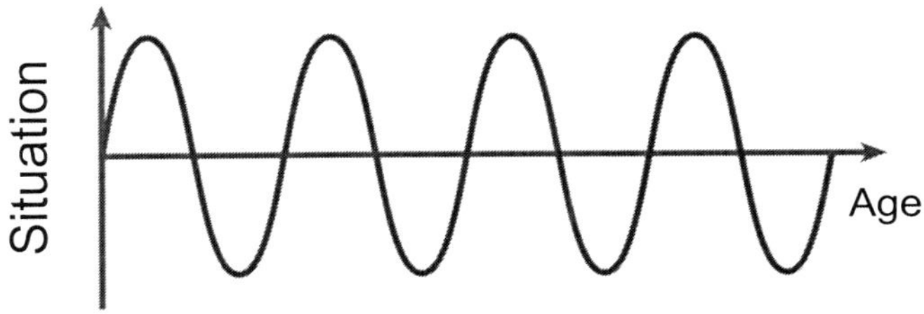

Sometimes you are doing well, and at times you are not, but how you tackle that in your mind matters the most. Our bodies have a physical and mental side. Since you suffer from physical pain, you can take medicines, visit the doctor, but with mental pain, it is much more difficult to get things under control.

To tackle mental hurdles, you need to understand the impact of positive thinking, creating a positive environment, and the concept of the body and soul, all of which are explained in this book.

Create a positive environment and vibration:

- Believe in the existence of God and the Supreme Energy Source.
- When you wake up in the morning, express gratitude to the Supreme Soul for giving you a human life and for the beauty of life.
- Avoid saying anything negative to anyone. Refrain from criticizing, whether it's about food, friends, partners, or managers. If you're struggling to avoid negative thoughts, try listening to meditative music or affirm to yourself that you are a divine soul, powerful, happy, and creating positive vibrations.

- When you start believing in the Supreme Soul and create a positive environment, you will automatically gain self-confidence.
- Realize yourself and who you are, whether you're a student, a working professional, or a businessman. If things aren't going well, for a week, forget about everything else. Take a break, start your mornings with positive affirmations, feel the presence of God, and express gratitude to everyone, whether they are your friend or your enemy. Remember not to attract negative vibrations. By doing this, within a week, you may receive guidance from God.
- If nobody is there to help you, just surrender yourself in front of God. Close your eyes, express your grief to Him, and request His help, guidance, and strength. He will be there for you. In scientific terms, God is the supreme source of energy, and we are small packets of energy. When you close your eyes, start meditating, and think positively, you will align your energy with the supreme source, and you will feel the presence and guidance of the supreme power.
- Gift positivity to everyone, and according to Newton's third law, you will receive the same in return.

WRITE YOUR GOAL AFFIRMATION HERE

Thank You Supreme Power for giving everyone the strength to bear difficulties and get the opportunities. To give everyone a happy and successful life. Thank You God for making this beautiful world where everyone helps each other, everyone takes care of each other.